The Complete Idiot's Reference Card for Teens

Have you lost track of the real you? You can, as the Bible says, sell your soul. The most common way to sell your soul is to simply misplace it. You lose track of your soul by being preoccupied with the demands of a fast-paced world and being too concerned about keeping up an image.

Take this brief reality check and see how you are doing *today:*

Reality Check

Complete these sentences.

1. Today, I have been feeling ...
2. Today, I have been thinking about ...
3. Today, my attitude has been ...
4. Today, I have been worrying about ...
5. Today, I have been really happy about ...
6. Today, I have been acting ...
7. Today, I have been honest with myself about ...
8. Today, I have not been honest with myself about ...
9. Today, I have pretended to be ...
10. Today, I have been true to ...

alpha
books

Spirituality Assignments

You just can't dabble in the spiritual life, you have to become a serious student. These are some assignments that I believe every serious spiritual student might want to try:

✧ Keep a journal. A journal is not a diary. It does not record the facts of your day but the feelings, thoughts, beliefs, and experiences.

✧ Make prescription cards. If you had a great day, write down why. Call these cards prescription cards, and whenever you get the blues, give yourself one of them.

✧ Keep a scrapbook of favorite memories. Attempt to remember what matters.

✧ Chase beauty around with a camera.

✧ Write poetry about Life's toughest questions and subjects.

✧ Write yourself a letter. Ask a friend to mail it to you in six months.

✧ Write a creed, a concise statement of what you believe.

✧ Write your own personal 10 commandments—not about what *not* to do, but about what *to* do and be.

✧ Write a sermon. Tell the world what you think it needs to hear.

✧ Keep a journal of prayers.

✧ Keep a journal of favorite quotes.

✧ Read a devotional book or book of poetry.

✧ Read the writings of the mystics.

✧ Explore another religion. Develop an internal dialogue between that religion and your own.

✧ Interview as many people as you can, to find out what they believe to be the point of Life—their life.

✧ Try to artistically create a symbolic portrayal of what you believe is the point of Life.

✧ Attend a variety of worship experiences.

✧ Create a worship experience; invite your friends to participate.

✧ Create a worship experience with and for your family.

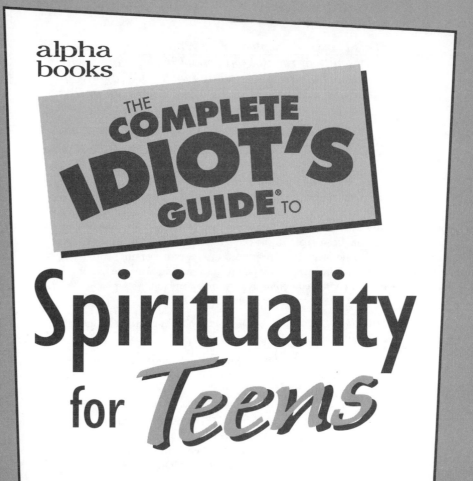

alpha
books

THE
COMPLETE
IDIOT'S
GUIDE® TO

Spirituality

for *Teens*

by Pastor William R. Grimbol

Macmillan USA, Inc.
201 West 103rd Street
Indianapolis, IN 46290

A Pearson Education Company

This book is dedicated to C. William Bennett and the faculty of the Buxton School in Williamstown, Massachusetts, for providing a safe place for young people to discover and uncover their own unique spirituality.

Copyright © 2000 by Pastor William R. Grimbol

International Standard Book Number: 0-02-863926-X
Library of Congress Catalog Card Number: Available upon request.

02   01   00   8   7   6   5   4   3   2   1

Interpretation of the printing code: The rightmost number of the first series of numbers is the year of the book's printing; the rightmost number of the second series of numbers is the number of the book's printing. For example, a printing code of 00-1 shows that the first printing occurred in 2000.

Printed in the United States of America

Note: This publication contains the opinions and ideas of its author. It is intended to provide helpful and informative material on the subject matter covered. It is sold with the understanding that the author and publisher are not engaged in rendering professional services in the book. If the reader requires personal assistance or advice, a competent professional should be consulted.

The author and publisher specifically disclaim any responsibility for any liability, loss, or risk, personal or otherwise, which is incurred as a consequence, directly or indirectly, of the use and application of any of the contents of this book.

Publisher
Marie Butler-Knight

Product Manager
Phil Kitchel

Managing Editor
Cari Luna

Acquisitions/Development Editor
Amy Zavatto

Production Editor
Christy Wagner

Copy Editor
Krista Hansing

Illustrator
Jody Schaeffer

Cover Designer
Dan Armstrong

Book Designer
Gary Adair

Indexer
Lisa Wilson

Layout/Proofreading
Darin Crone
Steve Geiselman
Bob LaRoche

Contents at a Glance

Contents

Foreword

Before my children entered their teens, I had a single, simple goal to help ensure my success as a father. Ideally, only one of my four children would be going through a crisis at any given time. Thus freed to devote my full attention, together we could surely resolve the problem. This worked for years. Some weeks were even crisis-free. Then my four children became teenagers. Now my goal is this: I pray that at least one of the four will not be going through a crisis at any given time. This is for my benefit as much as theirs. Otherwise, and with ample evidence, I would feel like a complete failure as a father!

The Chinese ideogram for "crisis" juxtaposes two ideographs (or word pictures): "danger" and "opportunity." I try to remind myself and my children of this, especially when we get too caught up with the danger part. When I lose my sense of proportion, as I sometimes do, I at least know enough to turn to others for guidance. Tops on my list is Pastor Bill Grimbol. He has an uncanny knack for seeing the "opportunity" side of the teenage experience. The last time I went to Bill, he left me feeling proud of one of my sons for the very thing that had distressed me. "He's on a spiritual adventure. You might not have chosen that exact path, but he's growing every day. He's a strong, independent-minded kid on a search. He needs your love and guidance, not your panic and fear. Stay in play with him, not against him. And remember one more thing: What were you doing and thinking when you were 16?"

This book is for my children, not for me, but as I read it I wished that when I was 16 Bill might have been there for me. His nearly 30 years as a youth counselor shine through on almost every page. As with many other books in the *Complete Idiot's Guide* series, Bill's *The Complete Idiot's Guide to Spirituality for Teens* is for idiots only in the ancient Greek root sense of the word, "idiotes," the people, the individuals, literally the "laypeople." It is an everyman book written expressly, thoughtfully, and passionately for teenagers. None will agree with every point Bill has to make, but I can not imagine any young person reading this book and walking away without the conviction that Bill is on their side.

During the course of a single tragic month this year, Bill lost both his father and his wife. Shortly thereafter I encountered him in a diner on Shelter Island having dinner with a teenager struggling as much with meaning as he was with school. A pastor myself, I was at first amazed that in his own time of need, Bill had so much left over for others. I shouldn't have been surprised. Bill Grimbol walks the walk as well as he talks the talk. From my own children I have learned that nothing is more important. As Thomas Jefferson once said, "It is through our deeds, not our words, that our religion must be read." The words in this book are great. The deeds behind them make them real.

Forrest Church
All Souls Church
New York City

Forrest Church is the author of many books, most recently *Lifecraft: the Art of Living in the Everyday.*

Introduction

At a recent meeting of my youth group, I asked them to define the word "spirituality" for me. For a few minutes I felt like I was moderating the first official meeting of Mutes Anonymous. Faces were blank. Mouths were closed. The silence was deafening.

Finally, Kevin, our youth group president, spoke. To be honest, I gave him a nasty glare that was his clue to at least say something—anything.

"Spirituality is, um, like, um, sitting under a tree all day long, and a, um, thinking about love and beauty type stuff." Kevin grinned and shrugged his shoulders, and the other 20+ teenagers laughed.

"That's right!" I blurted.

"Say what?" Kevin responded with wide eyes.

"You are right, or at least you are headed in the right direction. Think of spirituality as a beautiful white sand beach. Well, sitting under a tree contemplating beauty and love is one grain of sand on that beach."

"Just one?"

"Okay, I'll give you two, but they definitely belong to that beach."

On a whim, I led the group outside to a cluster of trees behind the church. I asked the group to be seated in a circle and to be quiet. I next asked them to just spend 15 minutes thinking about beauty and love. Just 15 minutes. Beauty. Love. Whatever came into their minds on those two themes.

At first they all looked like they were in pain, like they all needed to make a bathroom run. But soon the face contortions calmed, and I could see that they were relaxing and letting their minds free to wander and wonder.

After a quarter hour, I simply asked them to share their thoughts. The sharing went on for literally two full hours.

The comments made about beauty and love were quite profound. I think it is fair to say that not only was the group stunned by how much was actually said, and by *everyone*, but by their own depth and insight. It was a powerful experience.

They learned a lot about spirituality that night. Here are some of the highlights:

✧ We are all spiritual.

✧ Spirituality is a verb, not a noun.

✧ Nobody is stupid when the subject is spirituality.

✧ To be spiritual takes nothing more than diving in.

✧ Spirituality is not about answers.

✧ Spirituality is about asking the right questions.

✧ We know more than we think.

✧ There is no real reason to be afraid of spiritual sharing, because what we tend to think of as private is also the most general—it is what we have in common.

✧ Hidden deep inside us is a pretty wise and wonder-filled soul.

Spirituality. How does that word make *you* feel? What do you think when someone uses the word in conversation? Do you experience the concept as strange or weird? Do the kids who talk about it often make you feel uncomfortable or judged?

How would you define spirituality? Does it make you uptight to be asked about your own spirituality? Do you feel clueless as to how to respond to such an inquiry? Have you ever asked yourself how you would describe your spiritual life? Do you *have* a spiritual life?

Spirituality is a powerful concept. The word alone can have some pretty explosive consequences. Even a casual conversation on the topic can quickly become anxious, almost brittle with tension. Most young people seem to either talk about spirituality as if they have all the answers, or as if they could care less. Unfortunately, the matter of spirituality tends to make most teenagers either passionately defensive or incredibly cynical.

Why is that? Well, spirituality is a subject that addresses not only what you believe, but, more important, how you see your world, your Self, and your life. Somehow, all teenagers seem to know that when you are talking about spirituality, you are discussing something that goes to the very heart of being a human being. The bottom line is that spirituality *is* about that which matters to you most.

This book is intended to show you that you are indeed a spiritual creature. Spirituality is not something that comes from the outside in, but is something you already possess. In fact, it is who you are. If anything, your spirituality is buried or blocked. Like the members of my youth group, you may often bury your spirituality under the relentless pursuit of popularity or power or possessions. You might block your spiritual side by refusing to be serious, or to break the surface on anything from a discussion to a relationship. By playing it safe, never digging deep, and sticking to Life's trivial pursuits, you need never enter the arena of spirituality. A good chunk of this book will be devoted to removing the "clutter" that leaves your spirituality in the sad state of *mess*.

This book is also intended to show you—the teenager—that in most respects your age is not a spiritual handicap. Spirituality is not the private domain of adults or the elderly. Spirituality is available to anyone who wants to dig down deep and uncover it. As an adolescent, you are in the midst of rapid physical and emotional change and growth, and the exact same can be said of your spirituality. Adolescence is a fertile time for becoming spiritual. Since most teenagers are instinctually drawn to new ideas and challenges, spirituality can become a rich adventure of discovery for you.

Spirituality is not feminine or masculine. It is not easier for girls than for boys, or vise versa. Spirituality is genderless and raceless, and I believe, creedless. Spirituality is simply how you learn that it is the will of God for *human beings to be human,* and sadly, how most of you spend much of your life trying to be anything but human. Male or female, youth or adult, spirituality is about learning to *celebrate* being human.

It is my hope that this book will help you unpack this marvelous gift called spirituality. It is a gift you have already received. It is a gift that is guaranteed to make you stronger, deeper, wiser, more insightful, more sensitive, and most of all, happier. Spirituality is the way you can learn how to enjoy your life. It is the means by which you will become able to cope nobly with Life's tragedies, traumas, and triumphs. I am excited to share this journey with you, as I know you will be stunned by just how much spirituality can transform the way you feel, think, believe, and behave. It can indeed make all the difference!

"I saw the light"; enlightenment; the infamous white light at the end of the tunnel: Light has always been intimately associated with spirituality. To be spiritual is to walk in the light. To be un-spiritual is to choose to stay in the dark.

During the course of this book you will see information boxes scattered about, and I have chosen to identify them with light-related themes. The only exception is "Bill's Bible," where you will have to trust my own enlightened selection of quoted material.

The information boxes will be labeled as follows:

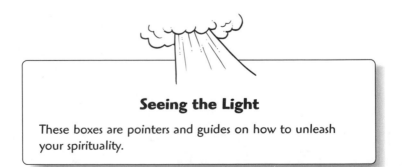

Seeing the Light

These boxes are pointers and guides on how to unleash your spirituality.

In the Dark

"In the Dark" boxes warn you of stumbling blocks and obstacles to spiritual growth.

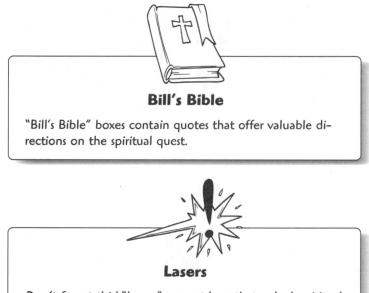

Bill's Bible

"Bill's Bible" boxes contain quotes that offer valuable directions on the spiritual quest.

Lasers

Don't forget this! "Lasers" present keys that unlock spiritual doors.

It is my hope that these information boxes can stand on their own: that by merely reviewing these boxes you will quickly be able to recall the themes and important points of the book as a whole.

Well, we're off. On our way. Together we will explore new lands and horizons. Together we will learn to recognize this "foreign soil" as *home*. Your real home. The distant land will be revealed as the yard next door. The faraway horizon will be as close as the end of your nose. You will soon come to recognize that the soul is not an alien planet, but a place as familiar as your own room.

Trademarks

All terms mentioned in this book that are known to be or are suspected of being trademarks or service marks have been appropriately capitalized. Alpha Books and Macmillan USA, Inc., cannot attest to the accuracy of this information. Use of a term in this book should not be regarded as affecting the validity of any trademark or service mark.

Part 1
Spirituality 101

Everyone has to start somewhere. Obviously, you're here because you want to dig a little deeper. You want to find out what this spirituality stuff is all about and why it's important to your life. Well, I've got news for you—we are all spiritual, and to be spiritual takes nothing more than diving in. Sure, you might be doing the doggy paddle at first, but after a while you'll get your stroke down and you'll be swimming along with the best of them.

You see, the thing is that spirituality isn't about having all the answers—spirituality is about asking the right questions. Think of these first few chapters as your life preserver, and I'm the lifeguard making sure you stay afloat. So come on, dive right in. The water's fine!

Chapter 1

Spirituality: What Is It?

In This Chapter

✧ What spirituality is

✧ What spirituality is not

✧ Why it is hard for teens to work on spirituality

✧ How you can begin to work on spirituality

Spirituality is impossible to define. I can't explain to you exactly what it is, how it works, or why it works. I can't give you 10 simple steps to becoming spiritual. I wish it were that easy.

Have you ever watched fireflies on a summer evening? The first firefly sighting of the season always feels like a miracle. When I was a boy, my grandmother and I would often sit on the front porch and hold a contest to see who could spot the most. I always won (I had a gracious grandmother). She had only one rule: I was not allowed to catch a firefly. She explained to me that a firefly was only beautiful when free to fly and light up the sky. She was right.

Spirituality is like that contest and its solitary rule. It is important to spot the fireflies of spiritual truth, but never to try to capture them. Fireflies in a fruit jar lose all their magic. Spirituality in the hands of someone who thinks he or she then owns the truth is dangerous.

I can only point *at* spirituality. I cannot hand it to you.

I can only help you to spot it. I can teach you how to get smarter in the "firefly hunt."

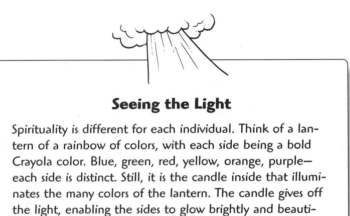

Seeing the Light

Spirituality is different for each individual. Think of a lantern of a rainbow of colors, with each side being a bold Crayola color. Blue, green, red, yellow, orange, purple—each side is distinct. Still, it is the candle inside that illuminates the many colors of the lantern. The candle gives off the light, enabling the sides to glow brightly and beautifully. Spirituality is that candle.

What Spirituality *Is*

I'm a compulsive list-maker. I wish I weren't. Most often, my lists are a complete waste of time. They always have too much on them. They are too demanding of time and energy, and too brutal in their lack of acceptance of flaw or failing. The problem with most lists is that they set up the expectation of perfection, which is always demoralizing. They are doomed to failure. Like most New Year's resolutions, these lists are quickly ripped to shreds by the sharp teeth of reality and humanity.

Lately, I have been trying to learn how to compose lists that are genuinely helpful. Lists that are not about *doing* but that are all about *being*. Lists that are not about the foolish pursuit of perfection, but about the goal of excellence. Lists that help me celebrate being human rather than feeling guilty about being one.

This book will be loaded with such lists. Because spirituality has much more to do with *being* than with *doing*, it is an ideal catalyst for a new kind of list, a new kind of challenge, and a new set of goals. It is my hope that you learn how to compose such spiritual lists—lists that help you to feel good about yourself and your life, and lists that don't make demands, but extend invitations.

So, with all this said, let me share a very important list, this one being what I think spirituality is:

✧ Spirituality is a way of experiencing life.

✧ Spirituality is all about awareness.

✧ Spirituality is about being fully awake to Life.

✧ Spirituality is mainly noticing.

✧ Spirituality will free you to see deep into the universe that exists outside, and, yes, inside as well.

✧ Spirituality is a way of looking deep inside yourself, others, the world, the earth, and even God.

✧ Spirituality is seeing and chasing beauty.

✧ Spirituality is a vision of the best you can be, the best we can be, and the best the world can be—heaven on earth.

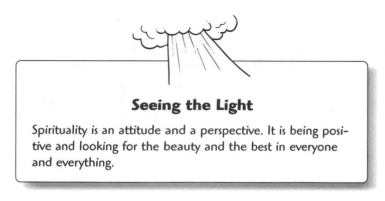

Seeing the Light

Spirituality is an attitude and a perspective. It is being positive and looking for the beauty and the best in everyone and everything.

Recently, I went for a short walk. I heard something. I stopped and noticed that it was a bird singing. I stood there for a moment and was delighted to hear a six-pack of birds singing in a nearby tree. I stood perfectly still and listened. There was a symphony of birds. To be honest, it was pretty much an unorchestrated racket, and I laughed at all the bird noise.

Now, those birds were singing all the time. They did not just start to toot and peep for my benefit. It was just that I finally noticed their singing.

Spirituality is like that. It is always there, like the beating of your own heart, but you seldom bother to notice it. You seldom stop long enough to hear it sing.

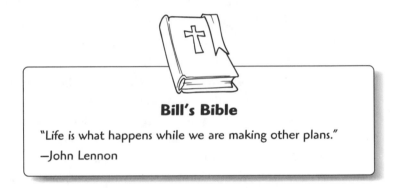

Bill's Bible

"Life is what happens while we are making other plans."
—John Lennon

At times you might feel like you are a spectator to your own life. It is as if you are trapped orbiting a planet called Now. Sometimes you might actually see yourself as if at a distance and wonder a lot of why's: Why am I saying that? Why am I acting this way? Why can't I show the *real* me?

I think that spirituality is stepping out of the audience and getting on center stage. It is about landing in the Now, and not orbiting. It is about knowing why.

What Spirituality Is *Not*

Usually, it is quite easy to come up with negatives. It can be far easier to say what something is *not* like than what it *is* like. In the case of spirituality, however, both are tricky and tough.

What is it that makes it so difficult to describe what spirituality isn't? Let me give you a concrete example as to why this is not an easy task. Although the Bible is an obvious spiritual tool, it can be used as a weapon to prove religious superiority, a detriment to spirituality. On the flip side, the Bible can be used as a vast resource of inspiration, not indoctrination—a very real spiritual asset. There is the crux of the problem. It all depends on the motivation of the user.

I think this is why many of you think many of the so-called religious kids appear to be the least spiritual. These teens often use their religion to protect and defend themselves, not to spiritually expand or mature. Frequently, religion can be constructed totally out of fear. A fear-based religion is one that talks incessantly about what *not* to do, the evils of others, the evils of the world, the myriad ways to gain entrance to hell, and the one way—of course, their way—to get into heaven.

Spirituality, on the other hand, is all about faith, which is expecting the best. It is not about fear, which is expecting the worst. Spirituality points out what you can be, the goodness in others and our world, and the many pathways to Heaven.

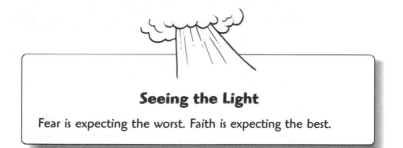

Seeing the Light

Fear is expecting the worst. Faith is expecting the best.

Fear-based religion is closed and unwilling to bend.

It refuses to change or adapt. It can become viciously defensive. It often cowers in a corner in fear, or must gather only with those folks who totally agree. Fear-based religion is dead certain. There are no doubts. There are no questions. There are no mysteries. There is only black and white.

Spirituality, on the other hand, is wide open. It is flexible and ceaselessly changing. It feels no need to defend itself, and it is always open to new ideas. It has great courage to explore differences of opinion and belief, and it truly celebrates such diversity. Spirituality is comfortable with mystery, embraces uncertainty, and seeks no warranties or guarantees. For spirituality, there are only many shades of gray.

Spirituality is definitely *not* based on fear.

In the Dark

Spirituality is not a contest or a competition.

Spirituality is all about expanding our capacity to live, love, and learn. Like the universe itself, you are created to keep changing, adapting, and seeking out the balance of compromise. Spirituality does not build up walls and barriers between people; it tears them down. Where there are locked doors, it replaces them with open windows. Spirituality has no fear of difference, or even conflict, but rather sees this as the context for great creativity and maturation.

Suffice it to say that spirituality is *not* …

- ✧ Becoming less loving and more indifferent or hostile
- ✧ Becoming less forgiving and more judgmental
- ✧ Becoming less tolerant and more intolerant

✧ Becoming less open-minded and more rigid in your thinking

✧ Becoming less willing to change or compromise, and more inclined to be fixed in one position

✧ Becoming less willing to admit a mistake and more inclined to have to be perfect

✧ Becoming less compassionate and more hard-hearted, especially toward those in crisis or need, the outcast, or those who are genuinely vulnerable

✧ Becoming less humble and more self-righteous

✧ Becoming less fascinated by life's many mysteries and more certain that you have it all figured out

Spirituality is *not* about anything that makes us less likely to love, learn, or live life to the fullest.

In the Dark

Beware of those who ask you to close your mind or grow calluses on your heart.

Why Is Spirituality Tough for Teens?

I have worked with teenagers for the past 25 years. I like adolescents. I don't enjoy adolescents who act like children, and I have a tough time with adolescents who try to act like sophisticated adults. I simply appreciate an adolescent who behaves like an adolescent.

Adolescence is a turbulent time—some might say it's even traumatic.

This is a short span jammed full of important emotional and spiritual tasks: resolving the identity crisis, learning the skills of intimacy, and declaring your physical and psychological independence.

I have found that certain qualities are characteristic of most adolescents. Although there are indeed exceptions to the rule—and you might be one of them—I have come to believe that most teenagers have the following in common:

- ✧ The need to be busy and on the go—or at least out of the house a good deal of the time
- ✧ The love of noise: talking on the phone, listening to music, going to concerts, and wearing headphones
- ✧ The need to hang out with friends—doing nothing, talking about nothing, and just hanging out
- ✧ The need to be part of the group, to belong and to fit in
- ✧ The tendency to talk before thinking
- ✧ The tendency to avoid showing feelings
- ✧ The tendency to avoid expressing convictions or beliefs, due to fear of either embarrassment or rejection
- ✧ A genuine fear of being truly alone
- ✧ A pervasive feeling of being phony
- ✧ A constant need to construct an image that makes you feel safe and secure

Bill's Bible

"Faith *is* much better than belief. Belief *is* when someone *else* does the thinking."

—R. Buckminister Fuller

With that said, let me share with you what I consider some basic features of spirituality, or being a spiritual person:

- ✧ Spirituality begins with *stop!*
- ✧ Spirituality requires slowing the mind way down.
- ✧ Spirituality often requires stillness and silence.
- ✧ Spirituality often requires you to risk not only being alone, but also being removed and separate.
- ✧ Spirituality asks you to think long and hard, to feel deeply, and to believe passionately.
- ✧ Spirituality invites you to get to know the *real you.*
- ✧ Spirituality is all about breaking down the image, taking off the masks, and learning to be rigorously honest with yourself.

As you can see, spirituality isn't going to be easy for you. That does not mean it's impossible, though. It just means that it will take some focused energy and effort to choose to work on your spirituality.

Sit Down and Shut Up!

If you recall from the introduction, when I first asked my youth group to sit down and be quiet for 15 minutes, I was met with looks of consternation. The idea of being still and quiet initially seemed too much to bear. I could almost hear their thoughts: "Why? Why bother? What is the point? I feel silly! This is stupid! What if somebody sees us?"

The resistance to stillness and solitude is often so strong that you might actually feel your body and soul squirming for release. The idea of choosing to sit down and shut up will feel like putting a plastic bag over your face.

Why is that? I really don't know. I do know that it doesn't improve as you become an adult. I still have to do battle with my need to be busy and on the go, the anxiety I feel about being alone, and the incessant flapping of my lips.

I still have to work to carve out time and space for my spiritual life.

What I do know is that spirituality requires solitude and silence. It just does. Without it, spirituality will wither as fast as a plucked flower.

Stop! ... Look! ... Listen!

Once you have let yourself physically slow down, stop. You need to let your mind and body calm down. Take deep breaths. Relax. Sometimes it helps to pray. Sometimes it helps to read something. All kinds of daily devotional books are available; if you ask, you will find some that are ideally suited to adolescence. You might give the Bible a whirl, but first ask your pastor or rabbi for some recommended selections. You might just simply choose to sit there and soak in the quiet. This is called listening to your heart.

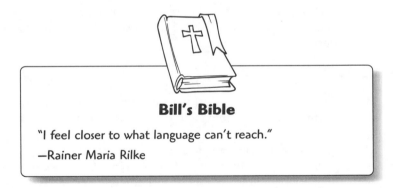

Bill's Bible

"I feel closer to what language can't reach."

—Rainer Maria Rilke

Somehow when you shut off the world, eternity is free to enter. Once you are quiet and calm, it is as if a whole new world opens up. You begin to notice all kinds of things: the way your body feels today, the smell of the air or the earth, the touch of sunlight or shadow, the vividness of colors. Your mind begins to clear. You become aware of your feelings and thoughts. You are in touch with your true self, with your soul, and with your God.

Spirituality is all about *looking* as if you were seeing something for the very first time. That means looking with reverence and awe. Look not for the flaw, but for the hidden beauty; and look with God's eyes, which means to look with love.

Spirituality is all about *listening* to your life. Listen to your heart, your mind, and your spirit. Listen to your losses. Listen to your heart saying a painful goodbye or mustering the courage to say hello. Listen to what you are dying to do and say and be.

My favorite teacher of all time was Miss Semington. She was a magical woman who filled her classroom with wonder and joy. She read to us every day, and that was my favorite part of each and every afternoon. I would lay my head on my folded arms atop my desk and let myself wander inside whatever yarn she was weaving.

Her voice was full and firm, and she animated characters with delight. Her old people sounded really ancient, and she could make you feel the wind or see the hidden valley. When she wanted you to listen, though, she would always say a very long "Shhhhhhhhhh. Pay attention ... plant this bit in your heart."

Spirituality is learning to be your own Miss Semington, to know when to say "Shhhhh" to yourself and to identify what needs to be planted in your heart. It means learning how to train your eyes and ears to pay attention to what matters and to what gives life value and worth.

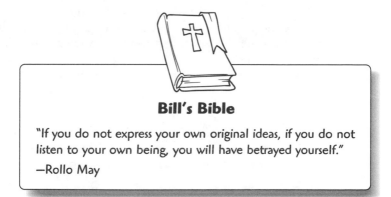

Bill's Bible

"If you do not express your own original ideas, if you do not listen to your own being, you will have betrayed yourself."
—Rollo May

A Spot to Stop

I have a place where I go to be spiritual. Sound crazy?

Maybe it is, but it works—and that's what matters. My place is a small pond, with a narrow path that winds its way along the shore. It takes 24 minutes to circle the whole pond; 30 in snow or spring mud.

I feel like I know every bush, tree, plant, flower, and animal that resides in the woods surrounding this pond. I know what colors the trees turn in autumn. I know where the lilacs secretly grow in spring. I know exactly the spot where the water stays warm enough in winter so that the ducks and geese can come.

Seeing the Light

A sanctuary is a place where you are free and safe. You need to find a sanctuary for conducting the "business" of spirituality.

As an adolescent, you will tend to enjoy change. You will get bored easily and will dislike routine. So, it is probably hard for you to understand what the big deal is about going to this puny pond. The big deal isn't the pond; it is what happens to me there. When I go there, I feel at peace. I go there to calm down, to get a grip, to lighten up. I go there to get my life back.

Spirituality needs a place to live, a home. You need to find a place that makes you feel relaxed and at ease, a place that just naturally calms you down. Maybe for you that is a hill somewhere, or a pier, or a clearing in a woods. Maybe it is your own room with the lights and the stereo and the computer off. How about the beach? A favorite tree or rock? A cozy chair or quilt?

Whatever the case, it must be a spot that invites you to stop, and that shuts out all the worries and fears of the world for a time. This should be a place that is old and familiar, but that enables you to feel fresh and new when you depart. This also should be a sacred spot where you find your self and locate your frazzled mind and harried heart. And it should be a place where you rediscover God.

Spiritual Mentors

Spirituality requires tutors, teachers, and guides. They can be young or old—black, white, yellow, red, brown. It does not matter whether they are Catholic or Protestant or Jewish or Buddhist. No degrees are required, nor even offered.

A spiritual mentor, however, must be someone you find to have these characteristics:

✦ Genuine and honest

✦ Accepting and affirming of you, but willing to correct or critique

✦ Worthy of trust and respect

✦ Insightful and wise

✦ Patient and kind

✦ Inspiring

✦ True to his or her own convictions, and who expects the same from you

✦ Comfortable talking about life's vital topics, such as love, forgiveness, and joy

✦ Capable of claiming his or her own failings

✦ Ready to change and grow

✦ Ready to forgive and to be forgiven

✦ Able to make the day better just by being in it

Are spiritual mentors hard to find? Not as hard as you might think. The key is to look in the obvious places: home, family, school, church or synagogue, the neighborhood. The best spiritual mentors are usually close at hand, but you may overlook them due to familiarity.

Look again. Listen again. I cannot tell you how many adults I know now recognize that the great spiritual mentors of their lives were their own parents or grandparents, a favorite aunt or uncle or neighbor, or a teacher who made learning fun.

Spiritual mentors are not necessarily extraordinary folks. They are usually ordinary folks leading ordinary lives. What qualifies them is not their fame or fortune, nor any degree or social rank. What distinguishes good spiritual mentors is simply their willingness to honestly and openly share their lives with you. The best spiritual guides offer a place where you are free to be exactly who you are, and in return, give back the exact same authenticity. Spiritual mentors don't lecture or scold, and do not advise or preach—they simply share their life's journey.

In my life, I have found spiritual mentors to be those few folks who have helped me uncover the truth: the truth about myself and my behavior; the truth about my relationships; the truth about my world and my place in it; the truth as I see it, hear it, and believe it; And the truth that is at the heart of my own personal God.

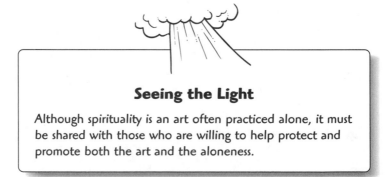

Seeing the Light

Although spirituality is an art often practiced alone, it must be shared with those who are willing to help protect and promote both the art and the aloneness.

But What Is It?

I am sure that at this point you are still confused. You may still be looking for a clearer, more precise definition of spirituality, or still wanting the 10 quick and easy steps to being spiritual.

That's okay—it is human nature. It is also a major aspect of our "quick and easy" American culture. Spirituality will never conform to those cultural expectations, though. Being a spiritual person is a lifelong process, and it requires some pretty demanding work.

Bill's Bible

"The Truth must dazzle gradually
Or every man be blind."

—Emily Dickinson

Spirituality is a process. It is a journey. It is an ever-unraveling mystery that is never fully solved. Spirituality seeks to clarify your thoughts, address your feelings, and claim your beliefs. Ultimately, spirituality is about locating the truth that I believe is planted deep inside you. A divine seed was planted within you at birth. Spirituality is all about bringing that seed to the point of blossoming and bearing fruit.

The Least You Need to Know

✧ Spirituality is something you already possess—it is a pure gift from God: grace.

✧ Spirituality is all about being aware—it is about listening to your heart.

✧ Spirituality is a lifelong journey of discovery. It is not about having all the answers, but it is about asking the right questions.

✧ Spirituality requires silence, solitude, and stillness. Try to find a sacred place that is all your own where you can tune out the noise and tune in to your own self.

✧ Spirituality needs carefully chosen mentors and guides. Often, these mentors are people you already know.

Chapter 2

How Do You Do It?

In This Chapter

✦ Why spirituality is an art—and you are born a spiritual artist

✦ How you can learn from the spiritual masters and practice the art of spirituality

✦ What spiritual clues your body gives you daily

✦ How to learn to trust your heart and your God

✦ Why becoming a spiritual artist requires that you spend time with your soul

Spirituality is a paradox. It is not something you can *do*, but is something you must learn to *be*. But if you don't do the work of spirituality, you will never actually become spiritual.

Say what?

Let me put it this way: Spirituality is an art. You are the artist. However, if you don't practice or perform your art, your skill as an artist will fade or disappear. What is probably the toughest point for you to accept is the reality that you are already an artist. The real issue is whether you will free yourself to create and learn to genuinely care about your creations. There is no bad or good spiritual art. There is only spiritual art or no spiritual art at all.

Think of the art of spirituality as having a palette, not with gobs of oily color, but rather with these essentials:

✧ Your feelings, thoughts, and memories

✧ Your hopes, wishes, and dreams

✧ Your prayers and your faith

✧ Your questions and your truth

✧ Your needs, wants, and yearnings

Spirituality is giving yourself time to brush these spiritual colors onto the canvas called life. As in all art, the goal will be to produce beauty—in this case, a beautiful life. Being a spiritual artist is to become a beautiful person, to develop a beautiful soul.

In the Dark

Beware of all those forces that keep you dealing with the things that truly don't matter.

Before I begin this section, let me clarify something. In trying to describe how to do spirituality, you'll see that I've compared it to several different things: coloring books, paint by numbers, and watercolors.

The use of these metaphors in discussing spirituality is essential, simply because it is impossible to capture spirituality in concrete tasks or concepts. Describing spirituality is like trying to explain love or joy. You can come close, but you never fully arrive at the answer. That is why the use of metaphors is so helpful. You have to approach spirituality like a poet—yet another metaphor!

Spiritual Artistry

Coloring in a coloring book is pretty boring because there is no freedom to it. You have no say in what you color. There is no chance to be original or unique. It's confining, restrictive.

Bill's Bible

"An artist has to take life as he finds it. Life by itself is formless wherever it is. Art must give it form."

—Hugh MacLennan

"Fine art is that in which the hand, the head, and the heart of man go together.

—John Ruskin

Art becomes dynamic and exciting when you are given a clean sheet of paper and simply told to create whatever you want. At first you may experience some anxiety—how do you choose from all the endless possibilities? Eventually, you settle on the idea for the picture and begin sketching it out. Then you begin laying in the colors, allowing your own personal style to come through.

Coloring book pictures may get gold stars, but they seldom get a mat or a frame, and they rarely are hung permanently on a wall. I have never seen one in a gallery or museum. I would never buy one to own.

Seeing the Light

Think of yourself as a spiritual artist, whose creations are worthy of being hung in the finest gallery.

Spiritual artistry is not like coloring in a coloring book. In fact, there are no coloring books, and no safe lines to follow or fill in. There is just the bright white parchment called your life, and the brushes of your heart, mind, and soul.

The art of spirituality is not about playing it safe. It isn't about calming down, but it's about getting fired up. It isn't about earning a gold star, but it's about creating something that you believe to be worthy of signing, matting, and framing.

Practice ... Practice ... Practice

When I was at St. Olaf College, I had an art teacher named Dorothy Divers. She taught the introductory course in drawing and painting. For the first eight weeks of the class, we drew bricks: big bricks and little bricks, and clusters of bricks.

We drew bricks in light; bricks in shadows; red, white, and gray bricks. By the end of eight weeks, I wanted to *throw* bricks.

Guess at who?

After eight weeks of learning perspective, shape, and form, Dorothy Divers unleashed us on the village of Northfield, to find and paint any building we wished. It was exhilarating to be freed from the brickyard. It was even more exciting to realize that my drawing and subsequent painting of a section of downtown was by far the best I had ever done. I remember being so proud showing it to the class. I hung it in my dorm room.

In the Dark

Don't try to copy anyone else's style. It never works, and you will never value what you have created.

The daily discipline of drawing bricks had paid off, big time. I had indeed learned perspective. I was aware of dimensions, shadows, and the impact of light. I knew how to show depth and distance. I knew how to reveal texture and color.

Spirituality is a lot like drawing bricks. It is a basic discipline that requires you to take time each day to ...

✧ Be with your thoughts.

✧ Know what you are feeling.

✧ Ask what God wants from you today.

✧ Ask yourself what you have learned today.

✧ Ask yourself how you want to change and grow.

✧ Appreciate and receive the gift of the day, no matter how small (maybe the music of birds or making someone smile) or significant (getting through a difficult situation or accomplishing something important).

The discipline of spirituality is in making time for your self, your soul, and your God. You can actually learn how to be a "time-creator." You do so by the choices you make, and by choosing to stop and think, and feel and question. You do so by being disciplined in your daily devotion to developing a stronger spiritual side.

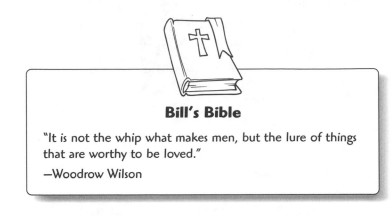

Bill's Bible

"It is not the whip what makes men, but the lure of things that are worthy to be loved."

—Woodrow Wilson

Study the Masters

Copying is helpful in artistry only when you are mimicking a master. The process of copying from a master will get you in touch with just how the master went about creating a masterpiece. You learn technique. You learn taste. You learn to appreciate the choices made in shape, color, placement, and style.

My favorite artist is Andrew Wyeth, and I have often copied his work. First and foremost, it has given me a deep appreciation of his technical skill in drawing; his attraction to somber settings and colors; his remarkable use of light; and his ability to capture a mood. My goal is never to reproduce his work, but rather to gain insight and understanding of his motivation and style.

Spirituality, as a field of thought, also has masters. By that, I mean that there are authors whose focus is on the spiritual arts. These are men and women who have worked long and hard to broaden and deepen their spiritual side. These are individuals who have practiced the daily disciplines of becoming spiritual. They have shown themselves to be individuals with a lot to say and wisdom to share. They may not have a huge audience, but it is a devoted following. They are also prolific and address spiritual matters from a wide range of perspectives.

Let me share with you my personal top 10 spiritual masters, as well as manuscripts I consider spiritual masterpieces. Now remember, this list does not include many unpublished folks and writers who have also achieved master status in my mind, nor does it acknowledge that masterpieces can also be found on film, on the stage, in music or art, in science and technology, in craftsmanship of all kinds, or simply by close observation of creation itself. I have limited myself to writers here, only because they are an excellent starting point for addressing the subject of spirituality. I also find these to be writers who are unusually accessible to adolescents. I strongly encourage you to pick up any book written by one of the following authors/spiritual masters:

1. Henri Nouwen
2. Frederick Buechner
3. Edna Hong
4. Archbishop Desmund Tutu
5. C. S. Lewis
6. Thomas Merton
7. Gandhi
8. Walter Wangerin Jr.
9. Tony Compolo
10. Madeleine L'Engle

I also highly recommend reading any of the following:

1. *The Screwtape Letters,* by C. S. Lewis
2. *The Art of Loving,* by Erich Fromm
3. *The Simple Truth,* by Walter Wangerin Jr.
4. *A Wrinkle in Time,* by Madeleine L'Engle
5. *Bright Valley of Love,* by Edna Hong
6. *With Open Hands,* by Henri Nouwen
7. *The Way of the Heart,* by Henri Nouwen
8. *The Alphabet of Grace,* by Frederick Buechner
9. *Wishful Thinking,* by Frederick Buechner
10. *Telling the Truth,* by Frederick Buechner

I would be remiss if I did not also call your attention to the poetry of Robert Frost; the radio broadcasts from Lake Wobegon, by Garrison Keillor; and all "Twelve-Step" material.

"The Twelve Steps" is a spiritual program utilized to battle addiction to alcohol, drugs, food, gambling, and smoking. I believe that the 12 steps given are quite simply one of the best and most practical guides to spiritual living.

Finally, the biblical parables and psalms are always a tremendous source of spiritual inspiration and reflection. Although the whole Bible can be thought of as a masterwork, I again recommend getting good advice on where to begin.

This is what works for me and is what I have found to be productive and helpful for the youth with whom I work. I am certain that you can easily add to this list, merely by asking and shopping around. The bottom line is that reading is a superb starting point for spirituality.

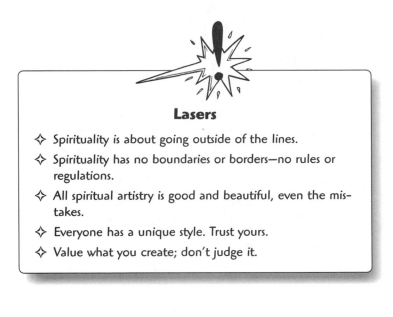

Lasers

✧ Spirituality is about going outside of the lines.

✧ Spirituality has no boundaries or borders—no rules or regulations.

✧ All spiritual artistry is good and beautiful, even the mistakes.

✧ Everyone has a unique style. Trust yours.

✧ Value what you create; don't judge it.

Paint by Numbers: Our Inner Body Language

After everything I've said about coloring and coloring books, why would I now recommend painting by numbers? Well, the sole valid purpose I can see for painting by numbers is to gain insight into the choice of color. You learn how the colors blend, how they can be warm or cool, and what colors are used to shade, darken, or lighten. Painting by numbers is a simple surefire way to learn about effective coloration.

In the same way, spirituality is a surefire way to learn about those experiences that give life vitality and color. Let me explain.

Your body will tell you when you are being spiritual or when a spiritual event is happening. Honest. You simply need to pay attention to your body to find out when you are getting near the truth, or when you have fallen smack dab on top of it. Your body will inform you when you are experiencing something that you need to note or have imprinted upon your heart. It will signal when you are literally being touched by the presence of God.

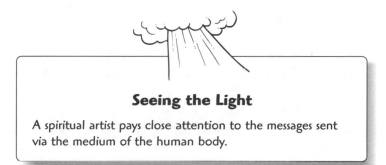

Seeing the Light

A spiritual artist pays close attention to the messages sent via the medium of the human body.

Let me share with you what I choose to call your body's spiritual "paint-by-numbers" kit. These are body signs and clues to spiritual experience. These are the "colors" that can bring your personal landscape or portrait to life. A good spiritual artist is someone who knows how and when his or her body is talking. A spiritual artist listens attentively to the following bodily messages:

✧ **Lumps in the throat.** These are filled with the grace of God, tenderness, mercy, and compassion. These indicate times when you are overwhelmed with just how good life can be or we can be.

✧ **Goosebumps.** You get these when you are coated with excitement, awe, or joy.

✧ **Tears.** You cannot lie and cry at the same time, so whenever you are moved to tears, you can be assured that the truth is close at hand.

✧ **Dumbstruck feeling.** Sometimes life's message is so poignant and powerful that you finally close your mouth long enough to hear the Word of God.

✧ **Breathlessness.** Whenever you experience raw beauty or truth, you go through a "mini-death." You are made aware that life is so precious, yet so swift that it is over in a blink. These mini-deaths lead to a rebirth of spirit. You regain your breath and your perspective on the sacredness of life.

✧ **Weak knees.** You can be sure that whatever it is, or whomever it is, really matters when you get weak knees. You are in the presence of love.

✧ **Stomach butterflies.** This is a simple cue that what is at hand is important—very important.

✧ **Spine shivers.** An electric current up and down the spine is a sure sign that life has taught you once again that you are not in control, and that you are definitely not God.

✧ **A feeling in the bones.** Your deep inner voice is begging you to trust this message.

✧ **A cold sweat.** You have just experienced something that is either too good not to be true, or a truth you can no longer avoid.

The human body is essential to spiritual development. It is the chalkboard upon which God, the teacher, most often writes. No spiritual growth can take place without bodily health. No spirituality can exist without paying close attention to how the body communicates with and for you.

In the Dark

You are often encouraged to treat your body as mere baggage, or as a carcass to which you need not show love and respect. Rather than being thought of as a "temple," many people treat the body like an outhouse. This is a sure way to stunt or even stop your spiritual growth.

One great way to get back in touch with the miracle that is the human body is to pretend that you are momentarily responsible for making it all work. You make the blood flow and the heart pump. You make the liver and lungs and kidneys function properly. You take over all the internal apparatus that we take for granted. It is stunning to realize the majesty of this thing called a body and to recognize that a whole universe exists within you.

Spirituality requires you to explore and examine both the universe out there and the equally significant one inside.

The Wisdom of Watercolors

Have you ever painted with watercolors? This is a magical medium. It is also quite tricky. I have come to see watercolors as a metaphor for spirituality. In fact, each time I paint, I not only learn something about life, but I also learn about becoming a spiritual creature. Let me share with you some of the wisdom I have gained from working with watercolors.

Go with the Flow

Watercolors, like spirituality, are rooted in risk. The risk is that you have no control over the water, just as you have no control over life or your soul. The risk is that any effort to control the medium ruins the painting. It takes a lot of time and practice to get comfortable with watercolors, just as it does in letting yourself become spiritual.

A good watercolor artist learns to let the water do the bulk of the work, and to allow the free flow of the water do its amazing artistry.

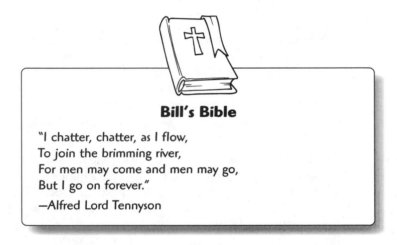

Bill's Bible

"I chatter, chatter, as I flow,
To join the brimming river,
For men may come and men may go,
But I go on forever."

—Alfred Lord Tennyson

A good spiritual artist learns how to let the *soul* do the bulk of the work, and to free the soul to inform and guide both the body and the mind.

A good watercolor artist is a master at using a variety of brushes to give direction and shape to the water and the paint.

The brush is used not as a weapon, but as a friend of the paint. The brush does not seek to dominate or control. The brush simply joins the watercolors for the journey.

A good spiritual artist uses a positive attitude and a spiritual perspective—seeing as if with God's eyes—to guide the soul toward maturation. Maturity is always the direction in which spirituality flows. A positive attitude and spiritual perspective serve only to keep the flow headed toward learning and growth.

A Lot of Gray

I have often noticed that the colors on my watercolor palette that most frequently need to be refilled are the blues and browns—the colors from which all grays are mixed. I have come to see that a bulk of every painting is made up of various shades of gray. Even if the color that leaps out of a painting is yellow or red, a vast majority of the painting is still composed of many, many grays.

Spirituality is all about life and living, and your life is also painted in shades of gray. Each day there may be some gold highlights, or a big dab of refreshing green, but for the most part your life is painted in the numerous tones of gray.

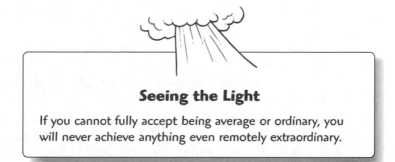

Seeing the Light

If you cannot fully accept being average or ordinary, you will never achieve anything even remotely extraordinary.

Gray is not a shocking color. It is a background color, a most basic color. It is the color of shade and shadow, and often is the color of earth, sea, and sky. Spirituality is also seldom shocking. Most of the time it takes place in the background, in the shadows of your daily life. Still, without those grays, the yellows, reds, oranges, and greens would fail to make their vivid splash.

31

Think of it this way: Gray is a good color for questions, doubts, and wondering—after all, it is the color of the brain. As I have said before, spirituality emerges from the fertile ground of questions.

The Whites

In the past two years, I had two small showings of my watercolors. One year the show was all of faces, and the last show was all of landscapes. The one comment I heard most often regarding my work was, "I just love the way you use white."

Now, this is both humorous and a bit annoying. There are no whites in watercolors. Whites are simply the blank paper shining though. Whites are the only areas on the paper that I have not touched or tampered with in any way.

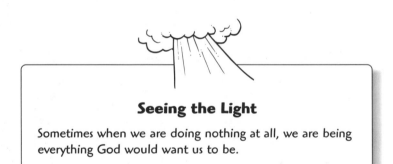

Seeing the Light

Sometimes when we are doing nothing at all, we are being everything God would want us to be.

Here, too, I have learned a most valuable lesson—a distinctly spiritual lesson. Life is often best when you leave it alone, let it be, and do nothing. This is why spirituality begins with a stop, as in when you stop trying to push or control. Just leave it blank. This is when the true natural beauty shines through—the true beauty of the paper, the blank sheet granted by a most gracious God.

Scratch and Scrub

When I was in the first grade, my teacher reported to my mother that I had used 36 pieces of printing paper because I

would not turn in anything that had an erasure mark on it. I
am a born perfectionist.

In the Dark

If you cannot admit to a mistake, you will never be able to
credit yourself for a success.

Well, when I started doing watercolors, I was crumpling up
expensive paper at a record rate. Finally, a wonderful mentor
said to me "Bill, you need to learn how tough watercolor
paper can be. You can scrub it. You can scratch it. You can
even erase on it. Learn to make your mistakes work for you.
Claim them. Celebrate them. Don't ever throw out good
paper. Keep working it."

Spirituality, like your life, is full of mistakes.

But the paper is tough. You need to learn to claim your mistakes, to include them as part of your painting, and to keep
on working until you get it right. Keep on scratching and
scrubbing. Don't be afraid to erase. Spirituality is not about
perfection—it is about celebrating being human.

Light and Shadows

As I have said, a bulk of a watercolor painting in composed
of gray. This is because most of what you paint is shaded, or
in shadow. A good watercolor artist, like a good photographer, has learned that what you are actually tying to capture
is light—those spots or spaces where the light dazzles and
shines. A good painting is one that lifts up the light, captures
it, and holds it up to view.

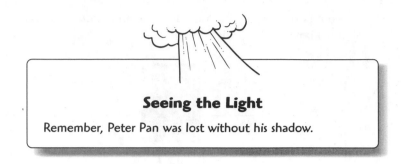

Seeing the Light

Remember, Peter Pan was lost without his shadow.

Spirituality is just like that: It is about capturing life's light and holding it up. Let the soul catch a glimpse and sing.

But—How Do You *Do* It?

I know. You still want something concrete. You want to have some specific things to *do*. Here is a lengthy list of spiritual starters. These are activities guaranteed to ignite the spirit:

✧ Take a long walk.

✧ Write down a list of your dreams.

✧ Write a poem, a parable, or a prayer.

✧ Float on water and watch the sky.

✧ Give an unexpected gift.

✧ Paint the sky—only the sky.

✧ Paint loneliness; do a sculpture of grief, or collage of anger.

✧ Ask someone to tell you his or her life story.

✧ Take a roll of film of your favorite things.

✧ Apologize to someone for an old wrong.

✧ Pray.

✧ Make a meal for your family, and serve it.

✧ Make a gift and deliver it.

✧ List your fears, and then ask yourself how you can overcome them.

- ✧ Make a new friend.
- ✧ Give a compliment.
- ✧ Sing for an hour by yourself.
- ✧ Take a long bath.
- ✧ Explore the woods.
- ✧ Canoe or kayak at dawn or dusk in silence.
- ✧ Swing with your eyes closed.
- ✧ Read the Bible aloud.
- ✧ Watch the sun rise or set.
- ✧ Play in the rain.
- ✧ Do a favor.
- ✧ Show respect.
- ✧ Include an outcast.
- ✧ Stop someone from teasing another.
- ✧ Read, read, read.
- ✧ Run into the wind.
- ✧ Don't keep score.
- ✧ Define holiness, joy, or friendship.
- ✧ List your good qualities.
- ✧ List your areas of needed improvement.
- ✧ Remember your favorite holiday experience.

Bill's Bible

"All the soarings of my mind begin in my blood."
—Rainer Maria Rilke

✧ Remember the time you learned the most about your self.

✧ Share your most embarrassing moment or your biggest disappointment.

✧ Write a letter to God.

✧ Write your own eulogy.

The Least You Need to Know

✧ Spirituality is an art—and you are a *born* artist.

✧ To be a good spiritual artist requires daily practice and willingness to learn from the masters.

✧ A good spiritual artist listens to the messages of the body: lumps in the throat, goosebumps, and spine shivers, among others.

✧ A genuine artist cares passionately about what he or she creates and doesn't ever throw out his or her art.

✧ To be a spiritual artist, you must claim your mistakes and include them as part of your painting. Spirituality is not about perfection; it is about celebrating being human.

Chapter 3

Why Bother with Spirituality?

In This Chapter

✧ How spirituality gives you physical energy

✧ The ways that spirituality frees you to be human and enjoy your life

✧ How spirituality gives you the strength to cope with life's problems and pains

✧ How spirituality will enable you to face death and dying

Last fall I took my high school ecumenical youth group on a retreat to Massachusetts. We stayed at a beautiful old inn, where we enjoyed huge breakfasts and late-night hot chocolates on an enormous wraparound front porch. We had some wonderful discussions about romance and love, saw a few movies, shopped at a couple of malls, went bowling, and drove daily, listening to the worst music ever recorded.

The last morning I took the whole group to the Quabbin Reservoir, a place of extraordinary natural beauty. The leaves were the color of fire. The sky was billowing with white, puffy clouds. The pristine waters, for which the Quabbin is famous, literally shimmered. I drove the group to the top of the highest peak, where you can see several states and some breathtaking views.

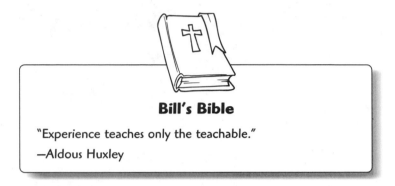

Bill's Bible

"Experience teaches only the teachable."

—Aldous Huxley

The group was groggy. It was morning, and sleep is not plentiful on any youth retreat. I told the whole group that I wanted each of them to take an hour alone. They could walk anywhere they wished. They could sit on a hill or by the water. They only needed to be alone for one full hour. I explained that at the end of that hour we would be having a worship service, and that the service would consist solely of sharing what the quiet time had taught us.

Once again I was met with screwed-up faces that shouted "Why are you making us do this? What's the point? Why bother? Why can't we go back and get a couple more hours of sleep?"

Catherine asked "Do you want us to think about anything in particular?"

"No, not really—whatever," I responded.

Tim then asked "Are we supposed to be looking for something? Is there something you want us to find? Is this like a treasure hunt?"

"No."

"Man, this is going to be one boring worship service, Pastor Bill," Kevin kindly added.

"We'll see," I calmly responded.

I watched as two dozen youth and a trio of adult advisers straggled off as if being sent to a labor camp in Siberia. Several kids looked back at me, waiting to see if I might change my mind, or if it was a joke. I smiled and waved.

They didn't smile. They didn't wave.

I must admit that the hour seemed long. I had a hard time trying not to figure out where everyone went, or what they were thinking about, or wondering whether the worship service really would be a bust. I would certainly not have much to share. I grew alarmed. This was supposed to be the spiritual finale to the weekend, an emotional highpoint, and all I could imagine was a flock of yawning youth.

The group returned, right on time. Everyone seemed happy. They looked rejuvenated. They were chatting nonstop and laughing. We headed for a ridge that overlooked a large cluster of birches, split in half by a splashing brook. The view of the waters and woods of the Quabbin was brilliant. We formed a semicircle, with everyone facing the fabulous view. It was a true scenic overlook, but this time we would not be overlooking—we were all prepared to look, to really look.

Bill's Bible

"A proverb is no proverb to you till life has illustrated it."
—John Keats

The worship service was extraordinary. The sharing was rich.

The spirit of the group was exhilarating. Everyone was genuine, honest, and real. Everyone listened to one another— really listened. We talked about such important stuff: fears of failing, relational wounds and bruises, struggling families, things we were grateful for, hopes for turnarounds and changes, wishes for new experiences, problems that must be faced, and issues that required addressing. We also spoke at length about the raw beauty we saw. We admitted that we felt like we had seen God face to face in this beauty.

We even spoke about Christopher, a young classmate who had recently died from brain cancer. We spoke of his living and his dying, and the many lessons learned. We talked about our own living and dying, and about the life and death of those we loved.

All this stemmed from just an hour alone—no assignments, no directions given. We just simply trusted the watercolors of the spirit to do their miraculous artwork. We were all amazed at how easily we had delved into life's most complex and mysterious topics. We were stunned by how much was felt and seen and shared—how much was in there, inside us. We were flabbergasted at how natural it was to worship, when we were sharing our own experience of the Gospel truth.

What was most evident was the love we felt for each other.

That closeness felt like the crisp autumn wind that swept over that ridge—it was an intimacy, a sense of community.

We had done the work of spirituality. We had celebrated the true meaning of Sabbath. We had taken a single solitary hour to be alone with our souls and our God. The only work that was required was to invite the spirit of God in and to then play host for an hour. The spirit did the rest of the work.

I know that every youth at that worship service knew why we had bothered. They all knew the point of taking an hour alone. They knew the true purpose of worship. I could not have explained that to them before we did it, though; only after experiencing it could they understand. Most of spirituality must be experienced before it can be understood. In fact, all of it does.

Lasers

✧ God comes when God is invited.

✧ God enjoys a good host.

✧ A good host is welcoming to all experience.

✧ A good host is nonjudgmental.

✧ A good host is a good listener—to the heart.

✧ A good host is gracious and genuine.

✧ A good host does not try to control.

✧ Good hosts are unobtrusive—you hardly know they are there, but they are everywhere.

✧ A good host invites honest sharing.

✧ A good host enjoys the whole experience.

✧ God is the perfect guest.

Spirituality as an Energy Source

One of the things that struck me that day at the Quabbin was how a group of exhausted young people could spend an hour alone with their God and return so energized. Everything about their demeanor was different. Their eyes were wide open. Their shoulders were set back. They had a slight spring to their step. They smiled. They laughed. They were so chatty. What had happened?

Spirituality is energizing. What depletes your energy supply is not only having to be busy all the time, but having to maintain your image for the crowd. You are always worrying about how you look, sound, and come across. It is like being on stage all the time, and anyone who has spent any time acting can tell you that being on stage is exhausting work. Keeping up appearances is a real effort. Keeping your feelings and thoughts in check is rigorous. The plain truth is that it is one heck of a lot of work trying to fit in and belong.

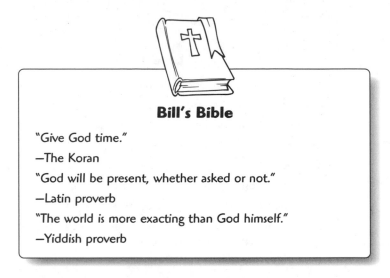

Bill's Bible

"Give God time."

—The Koran

"God will be present, whether asked or not."

—Latin proverb

"The world is more exacting than God himself."

—Yiddish proverb

When you are alone, however, you can drop the act. When you are alone, you can stop worrying about how things look. You can take off the mask and discard the image. When you are alone with God, you will know down deep that you belong and that you are already accepted, so you won't have to work at fitting it. You can relax. You can be who you truly are. You can just be. The experience of being at ease is renewing. Your energy supply just naturally rises, and you feel restored.

I am often asked whether I find the counseling part of ministry to be exhausting. The presumption is that it is draining to hear about people's pains and problems. The truth is that I find counseling to be not only rewarding, but also refreshing.

I find day-to-day chit-chat and gossip draining. I find all the cynicism and negativity on TV to be exhausting.

But talking honestly with folks about real-life issues, the day-to-day triumphs and tragedies of life, is an honor.

Spirituality is a real energy source. To get at it, though, you need to take time off from climbing the ladder of success, from proving to the world that you're a winner, and from showing that you are a somebody. When you spend time alone with your God, you discover that God has knocked out all the rungs to the ladder of success and has come down to declare that you are already a winner, someone very special.

Spirituality is grounded in *grace,* the awareness that you are loved by God uniquely. God respects and believes in you— you are treasured and adored as God's child. You are enough. Just think about how much human energy is wasted in trying to do and be and have *enough.* When you choose to spend an hour alone with God, you are reminded that you have more than enough right *now.*

Bill's Bible

"The trouble with the rat race is that even if you win, you're still a rat."

—Lily Tomlin

Spirituality as the Way to Freedom

Freedom is more a feeling than a thought. It is far easier to describe what freedom feels like than it is to explain as a concept. You know exactly how it feels to be free, and you know exactly how it feels to be enslaved.

Slavery—is that too strong a word to depict the opposite of freedom? Not at all. Slavery says it all and conjures up all the right images. To be a slave is to be trapped, treated with disrespect, and stuck in an unhealthy situation, to feel your sense of worth shriveling before your very eyes.

But how am I a slave, you may ask? Maybe you are a slave to reputation or popularity. Maybe you are a slave to image and looks. Maybe you are a slave to stuff. The root of all slavery is the loss of one's identity, the disappearance of the soul.

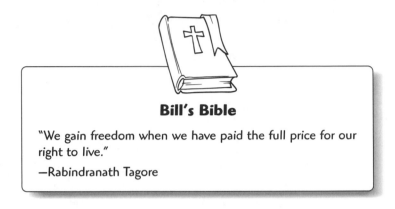

Bill's Bible

"We gain freedom when we have paid the full price for our right to live."

—Rabindranath Tagore

I think that most of the youth in my ecumenical group would admit to being enslaved by the popularity game. I believe many of them would admit to being obsessed with appearances.

I am sure that a few might even admit to being slaves to fashion, the ideal of being macho, thinness, romance, money, sex; or the party scene. One or two might admit to already being enslaved by alcohol or smoking dope.

Slavery feels like having a heart and soul in chains. It is a real burden to not feel comfortable saying what you honestly think, to keep your feelings in hiding, and to never be able to share your hurts or dreams. It is pure drudgery to go through each day trying to keep everyone but your self and God happy and to feel that you must live up to the expectations of others. It is hell to have to use a chemical in order to be relaxed and happy.

Spirituality emancipates the soul. When the kids gathered back for worship after being alone for an hour at the end of our retreat, they did so fully prepared to be honest, open, and real. Spirituality is getting back in touch with who you really are, the authentic self. No masks or games come into play in the name of pleasing other people. Spirituality is all about being true to the person God created you to be.

Ultimately, spirituality frees you to be human, to know that being human is just fine. When you are free to be human, you are also freed from the endless need to play God. This need to play God, or to be in control, is what bankrupts the soul. When you are forever thinking that you need no one and that you can do it all yourself, you squander the gift of grace that is offered to you every day.

Lasers

✧ You are free to be human.

✧ Being human is to be obedient to the will of God.

✧ Spirituality keeps you from trying to play God.

✧ Spirituality is the art of being on your knees long enough to know that you are not God.

✧ Spirituality is enjoying the chance to be *real.*

Spirituality as the Path to Enjoyment

Most of the youth with whom I work are extraordinarily busy people. I have come to realize, however, that they are not enjoying much of what they are doing. They are busy but bored. They are living at a frantic pace, which leaves them little time to appreciate the experience. Simply put, more and more teenagers are admitting to me that they are not all that happy.

To enjoy your life, you have to see a point and a purpose to what you are doing. You need to be assured that your efforts are worthy of the sacrifices you make. If you are just being busy to be busy, you will eventually feel like a person marching in place in quicksand.

Spirituality seeks to locate your point and purpose. Spirituality is about spending sufficient time with your soul to know just what it is that you believe yourself called to do and be. Not just ministers are called; everyone has a calling. You have gifts and talents that were given to you by God. The sole purpose of these gifts is to serve the God who gave them. The task of spirituality is to conceive and create this calling.

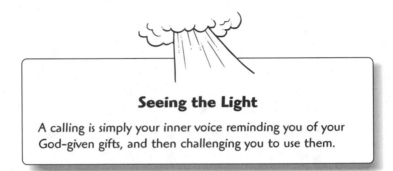

Seeing the Light

A calling is simply your inner voice reminding you of your God-given gifts, and then challenging you to use them.

Here is a good spiritual exercise to help you determine your own calling(s). Answer the following questions as candidly as is possible:

1. What are you gifted at doing?
2. What do you absolutely love to do?
3. What comes naturally to you?
4. What have you been told you are really talented at?
5. What can you do for hours and never tire of?
6. What are you doing when you daydream?
7. What gives you the greatest satisfaction?
8. What have you done that has had the biggest impact on others?
9. What can you not even imagine being unable to do?
10. What are you doing when you lose track of time?

Remember, spirituality is about freeing yourself to address life's most important questions—like, why you are here?

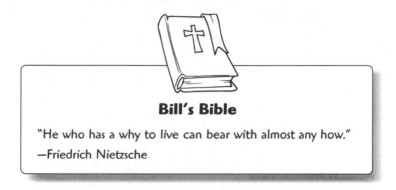

Bill's Bible

"He who has a why to live can bear with almost any how."
—Friedrich Nietzsche

Each day has a point. Every year of your life has a purpose. Part of your job as a human being is to reflect on the rhyme and reason of your existence. You need to think about what you are doing and why. You must review your past accomplishments and failures in preparation for actualizing your future dreams. Your calling(s) is a message given over a lifetime, and spirituality is the means by which you will figure out both the message and its meaning.

Joy will come to you when you believe that what you are doing matters. Joy is the result of living with a sense of calling and in a spirit of love. Joy is what happens when you see your life making a real difference. Spirituality claims joy as a goal.

Spirituality is coming to see that your life will never be measured by the width of your pocketbook or the length of your car. Your life will be measured simply and solely by the depth of your loving and the extent of your forgiving. In the end, all that will be remembered is how you managed to make the world a better place. The amount you have in the bank account is never carved on the tombstone. The tombstone carries only your name and the dates of your existence. Hopefully, your name will stand for wonderful things: generosity, kindness, compassion, integrity, or joy.

Spirituality requires you to ask tough questions, questions that can at first overwhelm you with anxiety and be downright frightening. However, if you choose to address these questions to the best of your ability, they will offer you the guarantee of satisfaction. It is no easy chore to ask yourself what you believe you are meant to do and be. Still, you just might find the answering of that question to be a source of lifelong happiness.

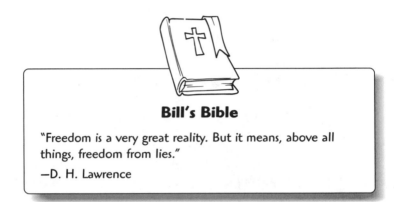

Bill's Bible

"Freedom is a very great reality. But it means, above all things, freedom from lies."

—D. H. Lawrence

Spirituality Helps You Cope with Life

Life is difficult. Adolescence is one of life's toughest times. There are no easy answers, and expectations run high.

Your peers can be ruthless judges. Every day is packed with potential hurt and heartache. If you allow it to happen, you can scare yourself silly. If you wanted to, you could easily come up with 10 good reasons not to get out of bed today. All things considered, it is pretty amazing that you function as well as you do.

Each of you has a coping reservoir. This is a tank filled with the ability to handle life's many ups and downs. You draw from this well to handle your disappointments and fears, anger and worry, guilt and grief. This reservoir is supplied with a limited quantity of God-given coping skills.

As you draw from the well, the coping supply begins to diminish. In the case of the coping reservoir, there is no underground spring to feed it. When the coping supply is gone, it is gone. When the reservoir is dry, you are in big trouble—ripe for emotional or physical disease.

It is your responsibility to keep the reservoir full, or at least near the top. And your spirituality supplies the reservoir. The one hour the youth group spent alone at the Quabbin Reservoir managed to fill their own coping reservoirs. That one hour alone had given them a renewed sense of focus. When we worshipped that day, we were sharing from a place of strength, a strength we had unleashed by having restored our spiritual balance.

Bill's Bible

"You only live once—but if you work it right, once is enough."

—Joe E. Lewis

Here is another good spiritual exercise for determining the state of your own personal coping reservoir; again, answer these questions to the best of your ability—be honest:

1. Are you tired a lot?
2. Are you sick a lot?
3. Are you eating all the time or not at all?
4. Do you sleep soundly, or do you wake up feeling more tired than before you went to bed?
5. Are you often on the verge of tears?
6. Are you irritable a lot?

7. Is your temper more explosive than usual?
8. Do you often feel like running away or hiding?
9. Are you drinking or drugging on a regular basis?
10. Do the obligations and duties of life keep increasing, but the rewards and gratifications keep decreasing?

If you answered "yes" to a good number of these questions, you can be sure that your reservoir is low. Remember, if it gets on empty, it will be even harder to refill—you just won't have the energy or the inclination.

Seeing the Light

Think of spirituality as a fire in a hearth. Your job is to keep the flames burning. What is the status of the fire in your hearth? Is it a roaring fire? A small, steady, glowing fire? A few fast-fading embers? Only you can build the fire back up. You possess the matches and the kindling. God gives the logs.

Spirituality Helps You to Cope with Death

Every day that you are living, you are also dying. That is true, but it's a hard fact to face. You will die. There is just no way around it.

Coping with the reality of death is one of life's toughest spiritual tasks, as well as one of its most maturing. Spirituality and maturity are often one and the same thing. If it forces you to grow and become the person God created you to be, you can be sure that it is something spiritual.

At a youth workshop I conducted for the Parish Resource Center, I displayed a lovely landscape painting to the group, unmatted and unframed. I asked them to take a long look at the painting. They did. I then placed a mat and frame around the picture, and asked the group to comment on the difference.

I was impressed with how quickly they saw what I had hoped they would see. They said that the mat and frame made the colors of the painting brighter, gave the painting dimension and depth, and made them feel as if the painting was inviting them in. One young man said simply, "It really brought the painting to life."

Death is life's mat and frame. It gives your life depth and makes the colors more vivid. It offers perspective and balance. It enables you to look deep inside. It offers wonderful contrast. It brings life to your life.

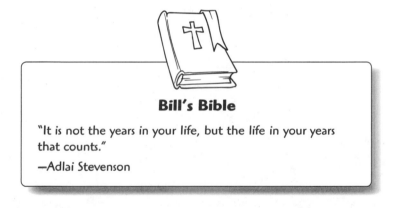

Bill's Bible

"It is not the years in your life, but the life in your years that counts."

—Adlai Stevenson

The Least You Need to Know

✧ Spirituality frees you to be exactly who God wants you to be—human.

✧ Becoming more spiritual will enable you to better enjoy your life.

✧ Becoming more spiritual will help you be able to cope with life.

✧ Spirituality helps make your problems more manageable by reminding you that God is on your side.

✧ Becoming more spiritual will give you the courage to face death and dying, and this will in turn free you to live more fully.

Part 2
Coming to Your Senses

The parable of the Prodigal Son, Luke 15:11–32, is a Biblical classic. In it, a son basically tells his father to "Drop dead!" He demands his father give him his inheritance so that he can get off the boring old farm and head out to pursue the good life, which unfortunately has nothing to do with goodness. He squanders his fortune in loose living and winds up at a pig trough—the ideal symbol for hitting bottom.

The story then makes a shocking turn: The young man comes to his senses. What does this mean? It means that he got back in touch with his spiritual self; to come back to the real person we so often leave behind. Coming to your senses is to return to common sense—it is heading back home to God.

What the young man left behind in Dullsville and on the family farm was his soul. He squandered not just his money, but the gifts of his spirit. His loose living was a letting go of everything that really mattered. All spiritually is about heading back home—back to the farm—back to the real you—back to the God who can be—and is—your best friend.

Chapter 4

Vision Quest

In This Chapter

✧ The ways in which you live much of your life in a fog, and how spirituality can lift it

✧ How you may be choosing to stay in the dark, and how spirituality can help you to see the light

✧ How spirituality can help you to hone your insight skills, or the ability to look inside your self, your life, and the mind of God

✧ What you can do to develop a vision of who you want to be and where you want to go

It was 10:00 A.M. My meeting was at 10:30 A.M., and I was easily 45 minutes away. This was an important meeting. More honestly, I thought I was important *to* the meeting. Whatever the reality, I was in a rush. When I hit the Sunrise Highway, a thick fog settled in over the road. I could not believe my bad luck. I was furious—which always helps. I slowed down to a crawl.

As I continued driving, a blue-haired woman who could barely see over the steering wheel passed me going 60. I stepped on the gas pedal and got up to 65 miles an hour in a fog as thick as pea soup.

Abruptly the fog lifted. The sun blazed. I was pleased.

I was also shocked by seeing just how much I had *not* been seeing. I had knowingly just taken a huge risk. If anything had darted in my path, or even slowed down, I would have had no way of seeing to stop. I could have been killed. I could have killed someone. All for a stupid meeting that could have done just fine without me.

Coming to your senses means being able to see clearly. In this chapter, we'll take a look at how spirituality can help you to cut through the fog in *your* life.

Driving Blind

Many of you knowingly live your life in a fog. To do so is just as dangerous as literally driving blind. The danger is not losing your life, but losing your soul.

Over the past 25 years of working with adolescents, I have come to the conclusion that most of you are highly prone to living in a fog. Although this is also true for a good many adults, it is uniquely true of today's teenagers. You are often clueless as to ...

✧ What you are feeling.

✧ What you need and want.

✧ What is bothering or upsetting you.

✧ What makes you honestly feel better.

✧ What is on your mind.

✧ What is going on inside your heart of hearts.

✧ What you believe in.

✧ What really matters to you.

✧ What you value and cherish.

✧ What you cannot live without.

I have also come to see that it takes very little time or effort for an adolescent to reclaim his or her soul. In just a few short hours, you can get back in touch with your soul, simply by *choosing* to lift the fog. How do you choose to lift the fog? Simply choose to take some spiritual time, which means ...

1. Stop what you are doing.
2. Find a safe sacred spot to relax.
3. Clear your mind of all clutter.
4. Focus on getting in touch with your thoughts and feelings.
5. Ask yourself spiritual questions.
6. Keep consciously slowing down.
7. Ask yourself what God would say, or think, or feel.
8. Be silent and still. Soak in the solitude.
9. Breathe deeply.
10. Listen to your heart.

Lifting the fog means giving yourself the time and space to see. To really see, though, you need to look inside. Seeing inside takes some time to focus.

I think of spirituality as akin to shooting a good photo. You first choose a good shot, but, most importantly, you have to make sure that the shot is in focus. A blurred photo is one that you will probably discard. To live your life in a fog with blurred vision is to discard your days.

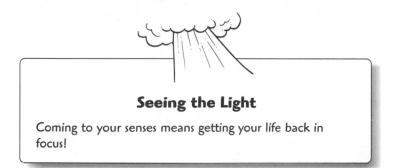

Seeing the Light

Coming to your senses means getting your life back in focus!

In the Dark

Frank was being unusually quiet. He was staring off during most of the discussion. He was normally not only a discussion leader in our youth group, but he also was the catalyst for open and honest sharing. Frank was fearless, was brutally honest with himself, and shared freely. Tonight, though, he sat passively, quiet, staring out the window.

After the youth meeting closed, I asked him to come to my office. I asked him to sit down. He looked at me, confused.

I asked him what was wrong. He said nothing. I told him that I had never seen him so quiet. He claimed that he was just tired. I told him I didn't buy it. I also told him that he wasn't leaving until we got to the bottom of what was bugging him. He looked relieved.

In the Dark

Secrets are never kept. They just keep us in chains.

We sat for 15 minutes in awkward silence, interrupted occasionally by Frank's reiterated claim, "I really don't know, Pastor Bill." Each time he said it, I replied, "If you don't know, nobody knows. We just have to take some time to figure it out."

Finally, Frank looked at me and said "I think it might be about my little brother."

"What about him?" I asked.

"I had to take him to school to be fingerprinted last week," Frank said. "It's a new program at his school just in case something bad happens to a kid. He is only six, and he had to be fingerprinted. I can't stop thinking about him being kidnapped or something."

There it was, a traumatic experience for Frank that he had kept hidden in the dark. This was a secret to his soul.

In the Dark

What you choose to deny winds up running and ruining your life.

Denial is a powerful force. It is most often a destructive force, and it was destroying Frank's day, mood, sense of security, and serenity.

We talked for over an hour about the crazy world we live in and about how sad it is that we have to fingerprint our children. Frank expressed a good bit of rage. We also spoke about the fact that his brother was safe and that we had every reason to believe he would remain safe. We talked about faith, which is hoping for the best and trusting that God will be there for Frank and his brother. We acknowledged that there was no guarantee, but that there was every reason to have faith.

We hugged. We both briefly wept. It had been an emotional conversation. It had been a spiritual conversation. I know Frank felt a burden lifted off his shoulders. By the time we walked out to the parking lot and our respective cars, we were already joking with one another. Frank's animated spirit had been restored.

We all keep things in the dark. We all hide our feelings.

Hurt, jealousy, rage, even joy and love—we all keep family secrets. Alcoholism, mental illness, physical abuse, incest, grief, broken dreams, broken lives, physical illness, depression, failures, sexual mistakes—the list could go on and on. Some secrets seem quite serious, while others seem quite silly. But to the person or family keeping the secret, it feels like life or death. The sad fact is that the keeping of the secret is the most lethal.

Here is a good spiritual exercise for taking a long, hard look at what you may be hiding. Again, take time to answer these questions thoughtfully and honestly:

✧ What hurts most to hear people say about you?

✧ What is your most embarrassing moment?

✧ How have you been teased?

✧ Does your family have secrets?

✧ What can your family not talk about?

✧ What is your worst fear?

✧ What is the biggest lie you have ever told?

✧ What loss pained you the most deeply?

✧ What do you consider to be your biggest failure?

✧ Who and what do you envy?

✧ When are you phony? Why?

✧ Who do you love so much it hurts?

✧ How have you sinned?

✧ How have you tried to hurt someone?

Seeing the Light

Knowledge is the effort to climb up the mountain to God. Wisdom is knowing that God will come down the mountain to you.

Seeing the Light

Over the centuries light has been commonly thought of as synonymous with truth. Not just a factual truth, but a gospel truth, a blazing truth, a truth that the heart cannot deny. We're talking about a transforming truth, a life-altering truth, and a depression-shattering truth. It's a truth that is sent by God.

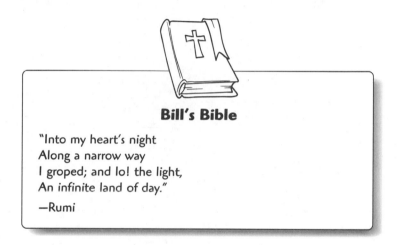

Bill's Bible

"Into my heart's night
Along a narrow way
I groped; and lo! the light,
An infinite land of day."

—Rumi

This light is not something that you can earn or achieve—it is something that you can only *receive*. It is a light revealed to you that always shines, even when you choose to hide in some basement cave. It is a white light, like the colors of a pinwheel being spun faster and faster, until all the colors miraculously merge into white.

My good friend Forrest Church, the senior pastor of the All Soul's Unitarian Church in New York City, tells of a majestic cathedral with the world's most beautiful stained-glass windows. Each of these windows represents a different religion. People come from everywhere to see the cathedral and its glorious windows, especially the window that represents their particular religious perspective.

As years pass, the people of the different religions begin to argue over who has the most beautiful window. The debates get heated. Tempers flare. Some call the other's window too simple, too grand, or downright ugly. A few folks even throw stones at another religion's window.

What all of them have forgotten is that it is the light, and the light alone, that gives these windows their beauty. Without light, there's no beauty. And the light all comes from outside—it does not belong to the cathedral, nor the windows.

Bill's Bible

"Rather than love, than money, than fame, give me truth."

—Thoreau

Seeing the light is to receive a message from God. Receiving isn't easy—well, it is, but you have made it difficult. You are bent on being so busy and doing so much that you seldom have time to receive anything. Plus, the idea of receiving makes you uncomfortable. Receiving means being dependent. Receiving is to be needy. You take pride in being independent and self-sufficient. So, you avoid the experience of receiving. You even feel awkward and embarrassed when you receive an unexpected hug or kiss or gift.

But you must face the fact that you are not independent. You are definitely not self-sufficient. In fact, if the world today is showing you anything or revealing any great truth, it is that we are all totally *interdependent*. I also believe that the significant spiritual revival taking place in our nation is first and foremost the result of knowing that we need God back in our lives—not an old-fashioned, old-time religion God, but the presence of a genuine higher power. Basically, we need to give our higher power some power.

Seeing the light is seeking the truth. You must actively pursue the truth. You must be rigorously honest. You must be willing to dig deep and find the truth of what you think, feel, and believe. Remember, the truth, like oil, will always surface—be patient and persevere.

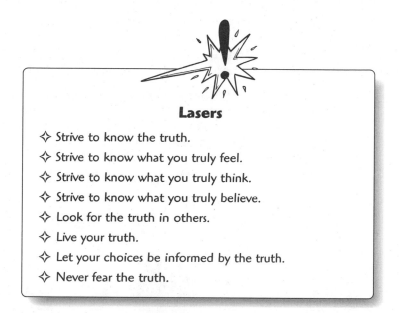

Lasers

✧ Strive to know the truth.

✧ Strive to know what you truly feel.

✧ Strive to know what you truly think.

✧ Strive to know what you truly believe.

✧ Look for the truth in others.

✧ Live your truth.

✧ Let your choices be informed by the truth.

✧ Never fear the truth.

Insight

Peter had changed. In the past he had always been gentle, shy, generous, thoughtful, and sweet. He had always been meticulously groomed. His clothes were not necessarily the latest fashion, but they were carefully chosen. He had been an excellent student and a reasonably good athlete. He was regularly given one of the end-of-the-year citizenship prizes. He never missed church.

His junior year, everything changed. His hair went spiked, and his clothes became funky and oversized. He pierced both ears. His grades dropped, and he eliminated sports and all other extracurricular activities from his life. He became loud and rude. He thought of himself as a chick magnet—which he never was before and, sadly, was not now. He talked loudly and often about partying and drinking and sex. None of it rang true. He wore T-shirts emblazoned with heavy metal band insignia.

Okay, what is going on in Peter's life? What is happening at home? Is he heavily into drugs and alcohol? I asked all the standard stuff, trying to figure out just what had happened to Peter to bring on such a sudden and total transformation.

The more I looked, the deeper I delved, the more confused I became. His family seemed fine, except terribly concerned about his behavior and attitude. His friends were still all the same good kids, and they reported that Peter rarely drank and had never, to their knowledge, touched a drug.

I could uncover no secrets, no divorce or family violence, no hidden alcoholism, and no recent loss of a loved one. In fact, I could find no traumatic event whatsoever. The more I looked, the less I found.

In the Dark

Think about how terrible it feels to have your efforts or love go unnoticed, and you will understand why noticing is such a critical spiritual responsibility.

While driving home from the movies one Sunday youth night, Peter was really carrying on. He was being loud and crude. I asked him to stop, and for few moments he would, but then it all would start up again. He had made up lyrics to a song on the radio, and the rest of the kids in the car were quick to let him know that they found them disgusting. Monica finally blasted him. "Peter, what has gotten into you? You used to be such a nice guy, and now you act like such a jerk."

"Well, at least you notice," Peter said quietly, and then stared silently out the window for the remainder of the ride back home.

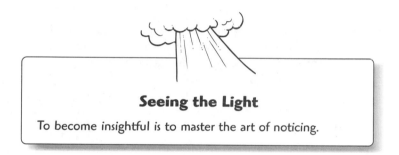

Seeing the Light

To become insightful is to master the art of noticing.

There it was, the clue. That was the peak inside Peter's soul and the glimpse of his pain. That single comment provided the answer to the question "What happened to Peter?" Peter had transformed himself in order to be noticed. We remembered him as a nice, quiet, shy guy. He remembered himself as someone who always fell through the cracks, who received little to no attention, and who was often either forgotten or treated with polite indifference.

In talking more with Peter in the weeks that followed, my insight proved accurate. Peter told me how tired he was of being the "goody two shoes," the boy everyone said they liked, but the boy who was never included in the parties or gatherings. Peter had grown resentful of feeling invisible and had made a conscious choice to be noticed. He made his point. There was no ignoring Peter anymore.

Insight is looking for the hidden truth. It is looking deep inside to try to uncover the real reason for feelings, behaviors, and beliefs. Just as in the case with Peter, insight often comes only for a moment—a gate opens, and, unless you are watching, you will miss your chance to pass through. An insightful person is someone who pays close attention and is vigilant in the search for the genuine article: the real self.

To become insightful is a goal of spirituality. For the most part, spirituality is the art of noticing. It is the discipline of a well-trained and focused eye. An insightful person will notice a look or gesture, hear a dropped remark or phrase, and catch the sigh or the stare-off into space. An insightful person is someone whose eyes are not only open, but whose heart and mind also are wide awake to the messages being sent.

You probably know somebody who you think of as insightful, a friend who somehow knows when you are down or in need of an encouraging comment. This is the person who never forgets to affirm your successes or to offer comfort when you've failed. Many times you might feel that your tears could roll down this person's cheeks, he or she—knows you so well. Spirituality asks you to become one of those friends.

Envision

When you were a little kid, one of your parents probably often said "Just where do you think you're going?" This was a question that was not a question. It was a statement. It meant "Don't you dare cross that street or leave this house." It meant "Don't go." It meant "You haven't a clue where you are going."

Bill's Bible

"Imagination is the eye of the soul."

—Joseph Joubert

Now you are an adolescent, and parents, coaches, teachers, and grandparents are asking "Just where do you think you're going?" This time the question is a question.

This is a question about your goals and plans. The problem is that most of you still don't have a clue where you are going.

To have a vision is to have a dream, a longing, a yearning, and a deep, passionate wish. Spirituality invites you to sculpt this dream. A spiritual artist spends ample time carving out the shape and form of his or her dreams. The artist gives these dreams detail and fine touches. I believe that you do have an answer to the question "Where do you think you are going?"—but it is lying shapeless in the basement of your soul. It is your spiritual responsibility to give that answer form and substance. Bring it into the light of day.

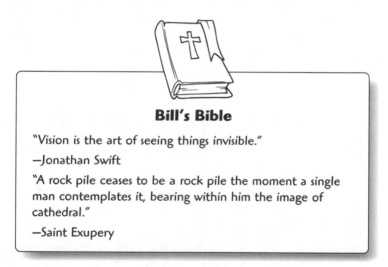

Bill's Bible

"Vision is the art of seeing things invisible."

—Jonathan Swift

"A rock pile ceases to be a rock pile the moment a single man contemplates it, bearing within him the image of cathedral."

—Saint Exupery

Here is a good spiritual exercise to strengthen dreams for the future. Like all good exercises, it will help develop the muscles of your imagination. Complete the following sentences:

✧ When I think about the future, I get so excited about ....

✧ When I think about the future, I get so nervous thinking about ....

✧ I have always wanted to be ....

✧ I have always had a secret fantasy to ....

✧ I cannot imagine my future without ....

✧ I think every person is put on this Earth to accomplish ....

✧ I just want one chance to try ....

✧ I think my future success is dependent upon my ....

✧ I hope I will always be ....

✧ I hope I will never be ....

✧ The single wish I most hope will come true is ....

Do this exercise every three months for a year.

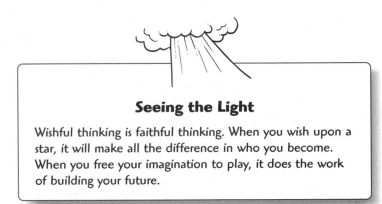

Seeing the Light

Wishful thinking is faithful thinking. When you wish upon a star, it will make all the difference in who you become. When you free your imagination to play, it does the work of building your future.

Blinded by the Light

The ecumenical youth group had gone to a Saturday afternoon performance of the play *Rent* in New York City. It is an astonishing piece of theatre, and the kids were mesmerized. While we were in the theatre, probably three to four wet white inches of snow had fallen outside. Everything was covered in it, like a clean sheet stretched tightly on a bed. The sky was blue and the sun brilliant. We all had to cover our eyes because the sun and snow were just too dazzling to behold.

Like the bright, white snow on that sunny day, there will be times that you have a hard time seeing. You may not be ready to know the truth, or you might be physically and emotionally unable to receive a blatantly honest message.

I think of spirituality as the endless process of getting you ready to handle the truth. Spirituality is the expansion of your awareness. You learn to see more and more. You learn how to look inside. You free your imagination to create visions of better tomorrows. You see deeper, farther, and with greater clarity. Spirituality is a recipe that asks you to slowly add more light. As the light increases, so does your awareness and your consciousness. This recipe must be followed closely, because to simply dump in all the light at one time can keep the ingredients from blending properly. Too much light at the wrong time can ruin the recipe—it can scare you off from even trying to see the truth.

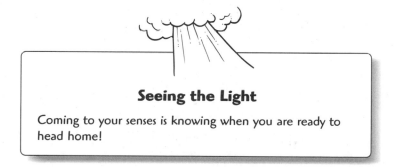

Seeing the Light

Coming to your senses is knowing when you are ready to head home!

The Least You Need to Know

✧ Living in a fog is dangerous—lifting the fog is a spiritual exercise that takes a strong soul.

✧ Choosing to stay in the dark leads to spiritual wilting.

✧ The human spirit needs the light of God's spirit to grow.

✧ When you begin to spiritually blossom, you will be able to look deep inside your self and the heart and mind of others—even God.

✧ You are spiritually called to envision your future so that you can work every day to actualize that dream.

✧ You are free to the degree that you are aware of the truth. You cannot change or become what you cannot see.

Chapter 5

Listening to Your Life

In This Chapter

✧ How to learn to listen

✧ Why becoming a good listener is vital

✧ How the heart and soul communicate with you—and why you need to listen

✧ The ways in which the Spirit sends messages to the human spirit every day

You hear naturally. Listening, however, is an acquired skill that is vital to your spiritual existence. There are reasons why you may tend to be a terrible listener:

✧ **Noise.** Everywhere you go, there is noise. Music is pumped into elevators and supermarkets. Your home is filled with the din of modern technology. You have countless conversations about nothing at all. Even your own mind functions like a jackhammer, pounding away in the secret language of stress.

✧ **Fear of solitude.** Only in solitude can you regain your ability to listen, but you are seldom, if ever, alone. However, many of you frequently feel lonely even though you are surrounded by people and voices and the necessary sounds of school, family, and community. Solitude creates the capacity to listen. Solitude gives you back your ability to hear the truth that speaks under and over the din of your daily life.

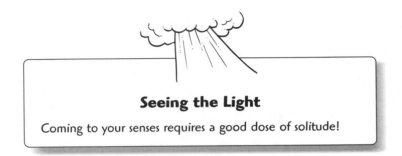

Seeing the Light

Coming to your senses requires a good dose of solitude!

The Sounds of Silence

I think many of you see life as an endurance test that nobody passes. I believe that God would like you to see life as a take-home test—a test that you cannot fail, and whose only requirement is that you just take it. It is a test where God is whispering the answers in your ears every day.

Silence carries the voice of your soul and your God. When the silence speaks, it is God telling you the answers.

The silence informs you how to cope with your feelings, solve your problems, and sort out your difficulties. The silence quietly speaks in words of wisdom, simply telling you how to enjoy your life and believe in yourself.

God does not speak with thunderclaps. God is not angry with you. God feels no need to shout in your ears. God just gently reminds you that you are loved, forgiven, and respected. God tenderly whispers hopes for your life. God strives daily to let you know that you already possess all the answers inside you, and that His/Her wish is simply for you to uncover and share those answers.

When it comes to spirituality, we are all equal. None of us is stupid when it comes to spirituality. Grace is an equal opportunity employer, so we all get the same answers. We all have already passed the test by simply choosing to take it.

Here are the answers I believe God is whispering in your ears each and every day:

- ✦ I created you to be you.
- ✦ I like who you are.
- ✦ I love who you will become.
- ✦ I expect great things from you.
- ✦ Greatness is measured in love.
- ✦ I forgive you.
- ✦ I expect you to forgive.
- ✦ You can make a difference.
- ✦ You are already making a difference.
- ✦ Relax—you are doing just fine.
- ✦ You can't fail, unless you don't take the test.
- ✦ I am so proud of you for taking the test.
- ✦ You passed!

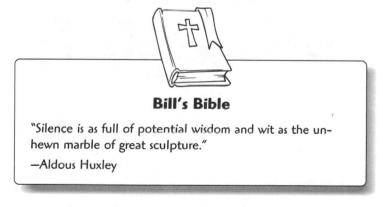

Bill's Bible

"Silence is as full of potential wisdom and wit as the unhewn marble of great sculpture."
—Aldous Huxley

Hearing the Heart

The heart also speaks. The heart expresses your emotions.

Your emotions are God's vocabulary. Knowing what you are feeling is to be informed about your relationship with God.

Bill's Bible

"It is only with the heart that one can see rightly what is essential is invisible to the eye."

—Saint Exupery

If you are feeling calm, creative, and centered, your communion with God is quite intimate. If you are feeling lonely, lost, angry, or hurt, you can be sure that you are feeling equally distant from God. If you are bored, anxious, or uptight, God is prodding you to make some changes, or to grow in some new and exciting ways. If you are worried sick, you are out of synch with God, and your relationship is, as the phrase suggests, diseased.

The heart tells the truth. The heart speaks softly and subtly. The heart beats with the rhythm of God's grace.

You need to take note of that pulse and listen not just to the beats, but to the silences in between.

Here is a good way to exercise your heart as well as to strengthen your skill in hearing it speak:

✧ What are you feeling right now?

✧ Recently, when have you felt the most happy? Why?

✧ What has been bothering you lately?

✧ What has made you feel content and satisfied?

✧ What emotion seems to haunt your days?

✧ What emotion do you feel to be out of control?

✧ What regularly irritates you?

✧ What do you feel a real need for?

✧ When and why have you been sad recently?

✧ What fear keeps gnawing at you?

✧ What do you worry yourself sick about?

✧ When do you feel most loved?

✧ When are you most loving?

✧ What guilts do you carry with you?

✧ What grudges do you still carry?

✧ What losses are you grieving?

✧ When was the last time you jumped for joy?

✧ What makes you get really excited?

✧ What are you enthused about?

✧ What are you dying to do or be?

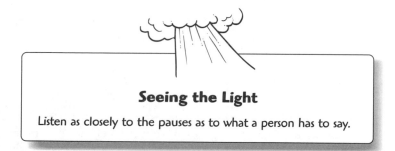

Seeing the Light

Listen as closely to the pauses as to what a person has to say.

When you lose contact with your heart, you are forced to pretend. You pretend to be happy, to be cool and calm and collected, and to have it all together. Your pretending is a performance that will eventually become a living lie. Living a lie is not only exhausting, it is also spiritually draining. A drained heart means a deadened soul. A dead soul is a sick, sad soul that cannot be creative, but only destructive.

You probably tend to want to know too much, but you let yourself feel too little. The reason for this is that your feelings tell a deeper truth that demands something from you. The emotional messages of the heart cut to the very core. Some pain and bleeding is always involved, but that's not necessarily a bad thing. A bleeding heart is a heart that feels God's pain and knows God's hopes.

In the Dark

If you can't admit to having a bleeding heart, you have yet to acknowledge that you are a human being.

Soul Sounds

The soul speaks, although it often has to shout to be heard. The soul shouts to call you to attention or to jar you loose. This is a voice that means business—the business is spirituality.

Listening to the soul is to listen to life itself. What is the earth teaching you today? What does the sky have to say?

The seasons? The rain? The daffodil or butterfly? The drought? What can you learn from observing your family, friendships, or the intimate workings of your school, neighborhood, or community? Are you listening to the messages that are being written on the wind? Do you hear the sounds of poetry and faith? Do you hear the echo of truth as it bounces off human hearts?

Life has a voice. It has a pitch and a tone. The voice of Life is vibrating all of the time. Can you hear it speaking to your heart and mind? Can you sense how it strives to inform you of what matters and counts? Can you tell that it is fighting to be heard? Even when shouting, the voice of Life must struggle to be heard over the din of the noisy world, which is forever preaching that happiness is to be found in money and accumulating more stuff. The voice of life seeks to say loudly and clearly that happiness is only to be found in living, loving, and learning with passion.

Bill's Bible

"Listen to your life. See it for the fathomless mystery that it is. In the boredom and the pain of it no less than in the excitement and gladness: touch, taste, smell your way to the holy hidden heart of it, because in the last analysis all moments are key moments, and life itself is grace."

—Frederick Buechner

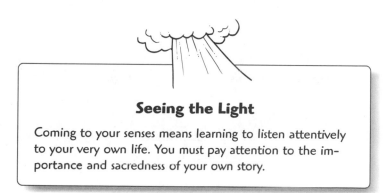

Seeing the Light

Coming to your senses means learning to listen attentively to your very own life. You must pay attention to the importance and sacredness of your own story.

Here is a spiritual exercise for the soul. It will take time to complete, and yet you will find that it is never fully finished. This is your chance to play Creator. Have fun trying to explain the many why's of the creation. Be creative—of course!

An Interview with the Creator

✧ Why different seasons?

✧ Why different races and languages?

✧ Why male and female?

✧ Why stars and planets?

✧ Why sun and moon?

✧ Why animals, fish, and birds?

✧ Why plants, trees, and flowers?

✧ Why mosquitoes and phlegm?

✧ Why volcanoes, earthquakes, and floods?

✧ Why ice and fog?

✧ Why a virus?

✧ Why do we age and die?

✧ Why pain and suffering?

✧ Why so many colors?

✧ Why war?

✧ Why evil?

✧ Why different religions?

✧ Why night and day?

✧ Why music, literature, and art?

✧ Why legends, fairy tales, and myths?

Seeing the Light

Coming to your senses means listening to your life, and knowing that every moment has a message, every day a declaration, and every year a sacred story to tell.

What's the Story?

Your life is a patchwork quilt of stories, myths, legends, fairy tales, fact, fiction, poetry, gospel truth, and history.

You may not realize it in the living or the telling, but all your stories have a central character and plot, a remarkably stable set of subordinate characters, and the traditional build-up, climax, and falling action. The thread that holds these stories together is made from your faith, hope, and love.

In America today, millions of folks attend anonymous meetings to battle various addictions, with Alcoholics Anonymous being the best known. Every day millions of people gather at these meetings to work at kicking their addictions. The program has had dramatic success, and the key to that program is the telling of stories. At each meeting, a person shares the saga of his or her own life and battle with addiction. The stories are straightforward and rigorously honest. No effort is made to impress or entertain. Facts, feelings, thoughts, and insights are all woven together into a simple fabric of truth. The group thanks the storyteller for sharing and for giving the gift of hope.

Bill's Bible

"Life is a handful of short stories, pretending to be a novel."

—Anonymous

Stories speak the truth. Stories heal. Stories create hope.

Take your own life story to heart. Share it when you can, and do so with humility. Listen to the stories of others, and garner glances of truth and grace. Recognize the story that God is writing upon the face of the planet each and every day, and see if you can distill a few drops of wisdom.

As a minister, I am asked to conduct many funerals. It is a sacred task. I always gather the family together to let them tell me stories about the person who has died. Nobody wants to hear facts at a funeral. They want to get a feeling of the person and his or her life; they want to feel like the minister really knew the individual who passed on; they want to feel as if the person is present and approves of what he or she is hearing.

These times of storytelling are truly wonderful. However, people are usually uncomfortable with how trivial the story may sound, but how important it is to them. Many times they are afraid to share the story that might be funny or tragic or downright embarrassing. But those are the best stories.

At the end of these sharing times, the family members almost always feel they have not shared enough, that there should be more, and that the stories should sound more important. Well, the truth is that each person's life has only a few important stories to share, and those stories are as familiar as nursery rhymes. What is truly important is the love with which these stories are told and the difference that these stories have made in people's lives. The significance of the stories is that with just a few, you can capture the spirit, the soul, and the genuine worth of the person who has died.

Seeing the Light

Think of yourself as an author and your life as a book. How will you keep it interesting until the ending? Make sure that you would not mind rereading it yourself.

The Least You Need to Know

✦ Listening requires solitude.

✦ Silence speaks in the voice of the soul and frees the
Word of God to be heard. It will give you all the answers
you need.

✦ The heart speaks your emotional truth.

✦ Emotions are God's vocabulary and express your relationship with God.

✦ The soul shouts for you to pay attention and demands
that you listen to the story of your life, as well as the
stories of others.

Chapter 6

Smelling Like a Rose

In This Chapter

❖ Why smell is a powerful and memorable sense

❖ How your sense of smell serves as wonderful metaphor

❖ Why you need to trust that you know what smells bad, and what smells wonderful

❖ Why you will have to do things that stink

❖ How smells offer signs and warnings, cues, and clues that should not be ignored

Smells are powerful and memorable. Think about some notable smells: lilacs, cinnamon buns, coffee brewing, chocolate, spring rain, autumn leaves, an attic, Grandma's quilt, a favorite perfume, a skunk, rotten eggs, homemade bread, home. Christmas trees.

Smell is probably the least noticed sense, but it's also the strongest. Smells imprint themselves on your memory and can call up a recollection on a moment's notice. Many smells are literally unforgettable, even eternal.

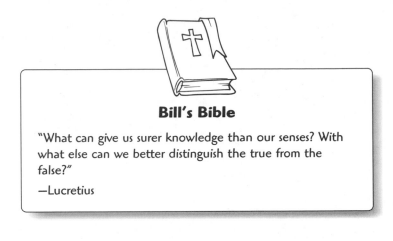

Bill's Bible

"What can give us surer knowledge than our senses? With what else can we better distinguish the true from the false?"

—Lucretius

You use the concept of smell to denote whether you think a situation is right or wrong. You know exactly what someone means if he says "This smells bad!" You even use smell to declare when something is evil: "This smells rotten to the core." Smell is a traffic signal. A good scent is a signal to go ahead. A bad odor says to proceed with caution. A stench tells you to stop, don't go there.

Smell is a wise judge. Smelling like a rose is to be declared a success. Smelling spoiled means something's rotten. To be called a skunk minces no words.

Let me continue to explore with you the power of smell, literally and metaphorically, to reveal the nature of things.

This Smells Bad

Animals use their sense of smell to sniff out food, sex, and danger. So do you. Your human sense of smell is not as highly developed because it is your most assumed sense. I am honestly not sure how much of your ability to smell danger is physical or how much is speaking metaphorically. What I do know is that you have an innate capacity to smell trouble. If you pay attention to this ability, you can develop a radar for detecting bad situations, relationships, or behaviors.

In the Dark

When a smell is overpowering, too sickeningly sweet, it is a sign of artificial air freshener—beware!

Tara was devastated. She had been caught stealing money from the cash register at work. She had not only lost her job, but she also had severely damaged her reputation and almost destroyed her parents. She was a pretty, smart, talented girl. How could she have been so stupid?

Tara was slightly overweight, an issue that had become obsessive for her—as is the case for so many young women. (This also stinks!) She had convinced herself that she could never land a boy, unless she was willing to make some big compromises. In this case, the compromise was getting her so-called boyfriend, Nate, the money he needed to get his recently totaled car repaired. Tara had explained to her friends and parents that Nate was trying to find work but was just not having any luck.

After her arrest, Tara came to my office. She sobbed. She called herself every name in the book. When she calmed down, I asked Tara what she had learned. She proceeded to tell me how many signs there were to her that she was being used by Nate, that she was more a wallet than a girlfriend. She said "Down deep, I knew the whole situation smelled bad."

Tara was right. The situation stunk. Her friends had tried to tell her about the bad odor. Her parents all but told her that she was choosing to live in a toilet. But most of all, Tara could smell it herself. Nate gave off the scent of a user. She just did not trust her own nose.

Seeing the Light

Coming to your senses means trusting that if something
stinks, you should not go near it—get out of there!

I believe that Tara really did learn. She now has a much better sense of smell, but more importantly, she is willing to
trust it. If a relationship smells bad to Tara, even a whiff that
she is being used, she's out of there now. She has developed
what is called a good nose for trouble.

Stinky Feet

Sometimes life stinks. At times you must cope with the
smelly parts of your world.

There is a wonderful story in the New Testament, about Jesus
washing his disciples' feet. Some churches today still perform
this ancient ritual during Holy Week. The difference is that
today's ministers are washing feet that are already pretty
clean. In fact, most folks who plan to participate in such a
ritual have scrubbed their feet raw before attending the ceremony. Such was definitely not the case in biblical times.

The people who walked the same streets as Jesus went bare-
foot. The streets were not highways for cars; they were lanes
for travelers and animals of all kinds. There was no highway
department to clean up the animal droppings. There was also
no sewer system. Walking those streets was a smelly under-
taking. You were destined to have your feet caked in dirt and
grime. It wasn't pretty.

It was the responsibility of a good host to offer a servant for
washing the feet of his or her guests. This was not a ritual or

ceremony, but it was done simply as a matter of course. Jesus' washing of his disciple's feet was his way of telling them that they must be willing to function as servants. They must not think of themselves as too good to kneel and clean stinky feet. Jesus was challenging them to be truly humble, to serve somebody.

Bill's Bible

"To serve is beautiful, but only if it is done with joy and a whole heart and a free mind."

—Pearl Buck

Spirituality is about knowing when to avoid what stinks, as well as when you may have to grit your teeth and bear the smell. Spirituality is walking humbly with your God. Humility is knowing that you are *not* God. Humility is given shape by your willingness to serve others. Now, not all service stinks, but a good chunk of the time, genuine service is a dirty, smelly, and thankless task.

As a minister, I witness folks dealing with life's "crap" all the time. At times it is hard to watch. Marriages explode because of affairs. Families are destroyed by addiction. People battle cancer, stroke, and Alzheimer's disease. Parents are forced to bury a child. Adolescents are paralyzed in freak accidents. The ravages of mental illness, the loss of a job or home, or the chaos of raising a child with serious disabilities take their toll. I am constantly struck by the great courage and dignity of so many ordinary folks. These are people who quietly go about cleaning life's toilets and cope with whatever life hands them. A good bit of it stinks.

Vomit

I hate to bring up vomit, but at times you will *have* to bring it up. The smell is awful. It is the fear of this stench that makes you try for hours to lie perfectly still in an effort to avoid having to do it. Of course, that never works. The only way you will ever feel better is when you get it up and out of your system.

Seeing the Light

Spirituality sometimes stinks—sometimes it has to. Sometimes the garbage going on inside you—the guilt, and grief, the raging fear, the molten hurt—all needs to be thrown out. Sadly, those you love the most sometimes must serve as your dump, just as you must serve as theirs.

Spirituality is not always pleasant or pretty. As you mature in spiritually, you will gain the strength to face tougher and tougher tasks. Spirituality can at times be thought of as a finger stuck down the throat. What comes up will smell bad, but you will feel so much better afterward. There are just some things that the human spirit is not meant to digest.

Whenever you choose to spiritually vomit, or even when you have no choice in the matter, you are getting up stuff that has gone rotten inside. Some stuff you may need to throw up:

- ✧ Family secrets
- ✧ Abuses committed against you
- ✧ Abuses that you have committed or are still committing
- ✧ Traumatic losses
- ✧ Times of great humiliation

- ✧ Major defeats
- ✧ Deep and haunting fears
- ✧ Perceived sins
- ✧ Sexual mistakes
- ✧ Hidden sexual orientation
- ✧ Rage

In the Dark

What stinks in your life? What situations or relationships smell bad? What scent is your first clue that it is time to leave?

Roses and Lilacs and the Sea

My father was English. The English have a fondness for front yard gardens, made up mostly of roses. My childhood home had such a garden. The roses were huge and in an array of shades: pale pink and yellow; white trimmed with red; the color of sunsets; pale, grayish lavender. The smell was glorious. Even to this day, the smell of a rose most reminds me of my childhood and my father.

I went to college at St. Olaf in Northfield, Minnesota. This is a terrific school with a splendid campus located atop "the Hill." The campus buildings always reminded me of castles, and I still think of the place as Camelot. In the lusty month of May, the Hill was covered with lilacs. The fragrance would drape the whole campus. The smell of lilacs still takes me back to St. Olaf, to a time filled with the magic of discovery and fresh love.

Seeing the Light

Aromatherapy is both a new and an ancient field. Through-out history, the power of spices and incense were used to create an atmosphere to welcome the gods. Now the power of smell is used for creating health and spiritual bal-ance.

I now work on Shelter Island, a quaint little island nestled between the South and North Forks of Long Island. From the very first day I moved here, I was struck by the distinct smell of the sea. It took time to get used to, but now I cannot even imagine being away for long from that sweet, salty smell.

When you are told to stop and smell the roses, you are being told to notice that which is too lovely for words. You are being told to slow down and savor the experience. Smells often can remind you of the best times of your life. For me, it's roses, lilacs, and the sea.

Here is a good exercise to help develop your *spiritual* sense of smell. Please complete the following sentences:

✦ I think it really stinks that my family ....

✦ I really stink at ....

✦ I have a good nose for ....

✦ I detest the smell of ....

✦ I love the smell of ....

✦ The smell of ... always reminds me of ....

✦ My favorite fragrance is ....

✦ ... is evil-smelling.

- The smell of ... calms me down.
- The smell of ... is invigorating.
- The smell of ... is upsetting.

Spirituality is about having a good nose not just for trouble, but for beauty and joy and love as well. Stopping to savor a luscious smell is an excellent way of slowing yourself down, of savoring and learning how to receive the gift of life itself.

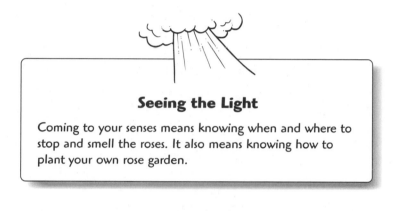

Seeing the Light

Coming to your senses means knowing when and where to stop and smell the roses. It also means knowing how to plant your own rose garden.

The Least You Need to Know

- Smell is a powerful sense.
- Smell often helps you remember what matters most.
- You need to develop a good nose for trouble and be wary of evil-smelling people and situations.
- Life can stink, and sometimes you must endure the stench.
- The Spirit will sometimes stick its finger down your throat to get up whatever is festering inside of you.
- Stop and smell the roses. This means that life at times gives off a fragrance that demands you to take notice.

Chapter 7

Getting
in Touch

In This Chapter

✧ Why being out of touch with your soul is to be lost and bewildered

✧ Why it is important for your soul to be in touch with your feelings, thoughts, and beliefs

✧ Why your soul needs you to be in touch with the lessons of your past

✧ Why being in touch with the world at large is necessary for becoming spiritually mature

✧ How to get your soul in touch with your God

In college, I read of a horrible experiment that was conducted in Germany during World War II. The experiment was executed at orphanages overrun with orphans and had to do with the impact of touch on infants. Some of the infants were held, rocked, and caressed. Some were not. All other factors were the same: All children were fed, received medical attention, and were kept safe and warm. The infants who were deprived of ample human touch died. I will never forget how startled and appalled I was by that result.

We all need to be touched. Without touch, we wither on the vine. It is touch that animates us, revives our spirits, and ignites our passions—of all kinds. Though I still think that experiment to be horrid, I cannot deny the profound impact of its results.

The soul also needs to be touched. An untouched soul will soon shrivel and die. The soul must be touched by thoughts, feelings, and experiences of learning. To touch the soul is to be deeply affected, to be brought to life. It is the soul that is able to be in touch with God.

Seeing the Light

Coming to your senses means getting in touch with all that is taking place outside and inside of you.

Out of Touch

Our Sunday ecumenical youth group was holding one of its traditional dinner/dialogues. This is where 20 to 30 youths gather and inhale a half-dozen pizzas, guzzle a slew of soda, and then take some time to talk. They talk deeply and honestly. They are open with each other. This allows them to get back in touch with their own hearts and their own friends.

One particular evening's topic was coping with fear. The discussion was lively. The group members had shared many of their silliest fears (rodents, spiders, ghosts and goblins), as well as their most serious fears: death of a parent or sibling, paralysis or a painful disease, a terrorist attack on New York City, a failed career or marriage. The mood wasn't somber, but it was intense.

Mid-discussion, Meg blurted "Don't you just love that new *Freaks and Geeks* show? It is just so funny. I love it. Did you see it this week?"

Hello! What? The whole group stared at Meg in disbelief. Where was she? Was she listening to anything that was being said? Was she being rude or just oblivious? The latter proved correct.

Meg was totally out of touch. She was deaf to what was being talked about. She was blind to what was happening in the room. She was not invested or involved in any way. She was out there someplace, orbiting the situation. Even the nasty glares of the group could not reel her in. She just looked at all of us and said "What?" To her, we were the guilty party. We were the ones who were out of touch with what really mattered—the last episode of *Freaks and Geeks*.

I am still not sure why Meg was so detached that night. Maybe she was just tired or disinterested in the topic. Whatever the case, she chose to be out of touch and to emotionally remove herself from the group. She chose to be spiritually oblivious to what was happening in that room.

Fundamentally, being in touch or out of touch is a choice.

Although your soul may call you to come back to your senses, you still have to make the decision to return. When you choose to be out of touch, you are choosing to be indifferent to the day, to those around you, to your self, and to God. Choosing to be out of touch is to lose yourself in nonsense and to run away from the reality of the moment. When you have elected to be out of touch, you have just voted for a deadening of your spirit.

In the Dark

Being out of touch is the spiritual equivalent of being unavailable—it's like calling in to life and declaring yourself absent.

Think of being out of touch as drifting out to sea. At first the drifting might feel relaxing. Floating can be fun. However, once you realize that you can no longer see the shore, the panic sets in. You are paralyzed by the fear of having lost touch with the land. The truth is that if you drift far enough out to sea, you can drown. To drift spiritually puts you at risk to drown in a sea of triviality, worry, stress, and the incessant pursuit of power and pleasure. What is drowning is your soul.

Have you ever been lost? Really lost? It is terrifying.

When you are lost, it is genuinely hard to keep your wits about you. When you are lost, you are out of touch with what is familiar, with all that makes you feel safe and secure, with home. To be spiritually lost is to have lost your soul—to no longer feel at home in your own skin, to no longer feel a part of God's family, and to no longer feel like you belong or fit in. To be spiritually lost is bewildering. It is to be caught in a wilderness of self-doubt and deep regret. It is to be found wandering in a desert of loneliness and fear.

Seeing the Light

Is anything so gut-wrenching as hearing the cry of a child who is temporarily lost in a store? Think of yourself as that child. Coming to your senses is to run to the rescue.

In Touch

To be in touch is to be present, available, and accounted for. To be present is a choice. It is to take the first step homeward. Being fully present in the moment, in the now, is a process.

Bill's Bible

"Now or never! You must live in the present, launch yourself on every wave, find eternity in the moment."
—Henry David Thoreau

It takes courage to make the choice to be present. If you are present, you must experience. If you are available, things will be expected of you. Choosing to be present isn't difficult, though; it is just tempting to choose *not* to be present and to remove yourself from the chaos and conflict of human relationships and to instead play it safe. However, choosing to be immune from the day's pains also means that you will never know its pleasures.

To be thought of as an "in-touch" person is to be paid a real compliment. It means that you are thought of as sensitive, insightful, compassionate, warm, wise, and centered—you're a doer, an individual who makes things happen. It means that when you enter a room, people are drawn to you; they stop and take notice.

To be thought of as "out of touch" is a harsh criticism. It means that you are thought of as cold, callus, dim, and scattered—you're a time- and talent-waster, a pursuer of the trivial. It means that when you come into a room, it is like five people left.

If you choose to enter the moment, you will be deeply touched. Every moment is precious, a gift uniquely selected just for you. Life is full of touching moments just waiting to caress you with compassion and squeeze the pain right out of you. Touching moments will bring you back home to life—they will tickle you pink.

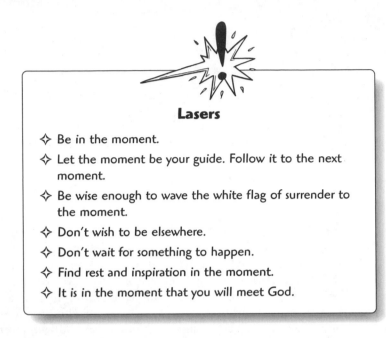

Lasers

✧ Be in the moment.

✧ Let the moment be your guide. Follow it to the next moment.

✧ Be wise enough to wave the white flag of surrender to the moment.

✧ Don't wish to be elsewhere.

✧ Don't wait for something to happen.

✧ Find rest and inspiration in the moment.

✧ It is in the moment that you will meet God.

Getting in Touch with Your Feelings

Feelings are God's messengers—they are there to inform us. They are not bad, good, or a sign of weakness or vulnerability. They don't need to dominate or control your life. Feelings only need to be heard and their messages received. Their information must be gathered if you are to be able to mature spiritually. To be out of touch with your feelings is to have lost track of your heart. As the Bible so rightly warns, where your heart is, you will find your treasure. To discard your treasure is to live a life that has no real value or worth.

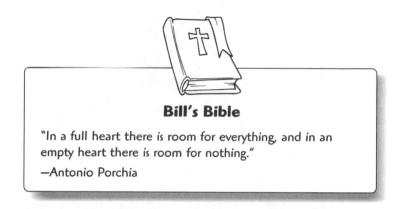

Bill's Bible

"In a full heart there *is* room for everything, and in an empty heart there *is* room for nothing."

—Antonio Porchia

Feelings are like the sea. They can be calm and tranquil. They can ripple with waves. The can be choppy and rough. They can be windblown into a foam-crested fury. The soul is like a ship sailing that sea. The ship will manage to navigate the waters just fine, if only the warnings are heeded. Some storms you cannot outrun, and the soul must know when it is vital to head for the safety of the harbor. God is the harbor.

Most of you live in your heads. You love to talk about what you feel, but you seldom let yourself *feel* your feelings. Being in touch is getting out of your head long enough to let yourself feel. As you work on this next exercise, take your time; let yourself feel the feeling before you respond. Notice what the feeling does to your body and heart and mind. How does the feeling communicate? What are the physical characteristics of this feeling? Use this exercise as a real means of emotional exploration. You are being asked to define the feeling and to share how it *feels* to you.

My Emotions

1. Loneliness: _____

2. Guilt: _____

3. Fear: _____

In the Dark

Is there anything worse than being told to stop feeling what you are feeling? It is like being told to hold your breath. You may be able to do it for a minute, but soon you will explode with the need to breathe.

4. Hurt: _____

5. Rage: _____

6. Jealousy: _____

7. Worry: _____

8. Need: _____

9. Anxiety: _____

10. Grief: _____

11. Boredom: _____

12. Joy: _____

13. Happiness: _____

14. Hope: _____

15. Love: _____

16. Stress: _____

17. Tenseness: _____

18. Yearning: _____

19. Desire: _____

20. Upset: _____

21. Discouragement: _____

22. Courage: _____

23. Want: _____

24. Disappointment: _____

25. Embarrassment: _____

Getting in Touch with Your Thoughts

Read over this parent and adolescent conversation. You can guess who is who:

"What are you thinking?"

"I don't know."

"You must be thinking something."

"No, not really. I'm not thinking about anything."

"That's impossible."

"What?"

"Thinking about nothing."

"No it's not."

"Yes it is."

"I do it all the time."

"Well, I wish you would start sharing some of that nothing with me."

"Say what?"

"You heard me."

"You want me to tell you about nothing?"

"Never mind."

The parent is exasperated. The adolescent is confused. Both were being what they thought was honest. The truth is that it *is* impossible to think about nothing. However, it is possible to be so disconnected from your thoughts that you are unable to claim them as your own.

I find that many of the youth that I work with are actually afraid to be intellectual. They don't want to come across as a geek or a nerd. This is equally true of young men and women. People don't want to read books or go to movies that might make them think. A conversation that becomes a genuine dialogue of ideas is thought of as too serious. A person who is attempting to tell you what he or she thinks is often thought of as having something to prove.

Bill's Bible

"It is not enough to have a good mind; the main thing is to use it well."

—Descartes

"I don't know" just isn't a good enough answer to "What are you thinking?" It is time you know. It is time you figure out what you think about that. You need to be proud of your thoughts. You need to claim them as your own and to speak them with clarity. You need to strive to be an intellectual. An intellectual is simply a person who has built up his or her mind, the same way that so many of you strive to build up your body. Intellectual fitness is just as vital as physical fitness—in fact, even more so. You must exercise your mind. Make it think. Ask it tough questions. Require it to do battle with doubts and confusion.

Defining concepts is an excellent way to stretch the muscles of the mind. Here is a list of some important concepts for you to define. Give yourself ample time to give your most intellectual response:

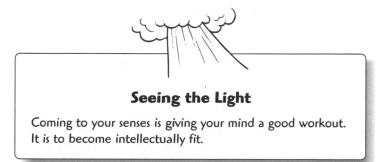

Seeing the Light

Coming to your senses is giving your mind a good workout. It is to become intellectually fit.

Intellectual Exercise

1. Justice: _____

2. Equality: _____

3. Integrity: _____

4. Dignity: _____

5. Maturity: _____

6. Leadership: _____

7. Honor: _____

8. Character: _____

9. Genius: _____

10. Confidence: _____

11. Will power: _____

12. Addiction: _____

13. Intimacy: _____

14. Attitude: _____

15. Respect: _____

16. Community: _____

17. Decency: _____

18. Morality: _____

19. Imagination: _____

20. Wisdom: _____

Getting in Touch with Your Beliefs

The previous week I had asked my ecumenical youth group to discuss their personal faith in God. To be honest, as they were being honest, they admitted that it was a relationship that could, at best, be called distant. God was more than an acquaintance perhaps, but certainly not a confidant. For most of them, God was like a distant cousin, someone they saw on holidays and at weddings and funerals. God was someone for whom they felt a vague connection, but with whom they shared very little.

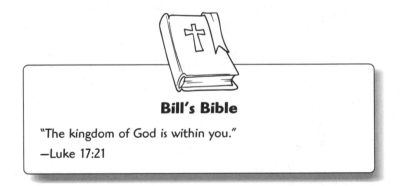

Bill's Bible

"The kingdom of God is within you."
—Luke 17:21

The very next week we were having a heated dialogue about the homeless. For the most part, the discussion was purely political, with many different opinions being shared on the topic.

At one point in the discussion, I asked the group to imagine that God was in their midst right now and to tell me what they thought God would have to say. The group responded without hesitation. They felt that God would have harsh words for such a wealthy nation that allowed so many of its citizens to inhabit the city streets. They believed that God would challenge us to not only find housing for these folks, but also to take them in ourselves, to learn to live on less, and to more readily share what we have. They were bold enough to say that God would call us spoiled brats and would tell us to take care of those who were the real have-nots. They were quick to point out to me, the minister in residence, that it was the church's job to lead the fight.

I reminded them of our discussion the previous week. I told them that I found it fascinating that the same group who had told me that they had a polite, cordial relationship with a distant God were now able to tell me what God would say, think, feel, and believe. How could this be? How could you not be on intimate terms with someone you claimed to know well enough to speak for? They were dumbstruck. So was I.

I would bet almost anything that you, too, have a much deeper relationship with God than you might expect. I would also venture a spiritually educated guess that your beliefs are firmer and more deeply rooted than you know. The fact is that you are rarely, if ever, asked to express your beliefs. Few opportunities are given to you to share your morality and ethics. Why is that?

I think it is because the adult population tends to be afraid of your questions, doubts, creativity, disregard for traditional authority, and often well-developed tolerance for diversity of opinion. Too many adults are interested only in indoctrination when it comes to beliefs and are terrified of you seeking to discover your own personal truths.

I think it is essential to your own spiritual growth to give yourself the time and space to declare your doubts, questions, and beliefs. Frederick Buechner was accurate when he called doubts "the ants in the pants of faith." Of the vital importance of the questioning process, Buechner writes, "To lose track of such deep questions as these is to risk losing track of who we really are in our own depths and where we are really going." Your beliefs can only grow stronger when they are given a chance to be expressed and, believe it or not, are nurtured by defending them against doubts and questions.

In the Dark

If you have been told what to believe and have had no choice in the matter, then it cannot be called faith. There must be a leap to faith, but when you are handed a faith and told that you have to believe it, you have been robbed of the joy of flying.

Spirituality is never about indoctrination. Nobody can pour beliefs into you as if you're an empty glass.

Spirituality is always about inspiration. It is the igniting of a fire within and underneath you. The flames of this fire will spark your interest and warm you to the passionate search for faith.

This journey of discovery that we call faith can indeed be the most exciting and rewarding adventure of your entire life. It is fine to ask for directions or even to purchase a map or two, but the trip itself must always be open to the spontaneous sojourn down a side road or an unmarked path. That is why they call it faith.

Define the following terms from the perspective of your own faith, and explain how you integrate them into your life and faith. Do not feel compelled to give what your family or church or synagogue would say is the right answer. If the Bible tells you that your faith will set you free, then don't wrap yourself tightly in the chains of doctrine and dogma. Let it rip:

I Believe Survey

1. Sin: _____

2. Evil: _____

 3. Heaven: _____

 4. Hell: _____

 5. Satan: _____

 6. Holy: _____

 7. Saint: _____

 8. Sacrifice: _____

 9. Service: _____

10. Religion: _____

11. Creator: _____

12. Jew: _____

13. Christian: _____

14. Cult: _____

15. Conversion: _____

16. Miracle: _____

17. Eternity: _____

18. Kingdom of God: _____

19. Adam and Eve: _____

20. Agnostic: _____

21. Confession: _____

22. Messiah: _____

23. Salvation: _____

24. Mystery: _____

25. Worship: _____

Getting in Touch with Your Past

Have you ever stopped long enough to really remember?
Have you ever asked yourself what your past has taught you
about life? Have you given yourself the time to reflect on the
most meaningful events of your life?

Bill's Bible

"Those who do not remember the past are condemned to relive it."

—George Santayana

Those memories that are painful to recall are the most crucial to your spiritual development. Pain is a strict but competent teacher. The lessons learned from pain are carved deeply onto your heart and mind. These are also the memories that you may need to vomit up in order to feel better. There is truly no way to get ready for pain. The best thing is to get through it and past it.

A big part of my ministry is to challenge people to remember. Remembrance is a huge chunk of the business of faith and the church. I try to encourage my congregation to remember what matters—to recount their blessings, learn from their mistakes, and remember what Christ has taught them. The church does not stroll down memory lane, but it reminds folks that the walk down the road less traveled will make all the difference.

Memory can be creative. It can also be a tremendous source of courage. Memory can restore balance, heal, and lead you into taking leaps of faith. Memory begets life.

Here is a wonderful way of learning how your memory can serve as a terrific tutor. Recalling favorite things is a way of informing and encouraging yourself to strive for more of the same. Complete the following sentences:

My Favorite Things

1. My favorite gift that I have ever received, was a ....

2. My all-time favorite teacher was ....

3. My favorite Christmas was when ....
4. My favorite birthday was when ....
5. My favorite vacation was when ....
6. My favorite memory from elementary school was the time I ....
7. My favorite childhood memory is ....
8. My favorite memory of my grandpa was when he ....
9. My favorite memory of my grandma was when she ....
10. My favorite memory of my dad was when he ....
11. My favorite memory of my mom was when she ....
12. My favorite memory of my family is the time we ....
13. My favorite meal I ever ate was ....
14. My favorite movie of all time is ....
15. My favorite song of all time is ....
16. My favorite toy was ....
17. My favorite adventure was the time I ....
18. My favorite neighbor from my childhood was ....
19. My favorite book of all time is ....
20. My favorite fairy tale was ....

This exact survey can also be done with the insertion of the word *least* so that you are asking yourself about your *least favorite* experiences—both can be quite revealing and spiritually beneficial.

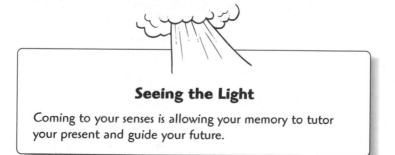

Seeing the Light

Coming to your senses is allowing your memory to tutor your present and guide your future.

Getting in Touch with Your World

Many of you have gotten to be real experts in how to ignore the world. You have no interest in politics, economics, or the workings of society. You have no awareness of other cultures or religions, or consciousness of any world beyond the confines of your room, car, school, and town. Is this you?

Many of you may find that you've created a private universe in which to dwell. You live inside a role: the prep, the jock, the druggie, the geek, the nerd, the headbanger, the skinhead, the born-againer, the young Republican, the young Democrat, the conservative, the liberal, the whatever. You live inside a romance, a computer, your music, your books, your sports, your TV programs, or the movies. It isn't all that hard to withdraw into a small, small world that is of your own making. Is this you?

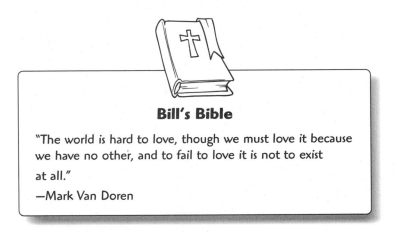

Bill's Bible

"The world is hard to love, though we must love it because we have no other, and to fail to love it is not to exist at all."
—Mark Van Doren

Spirituality must take place in the world; it cannot take place outside of the world (as far as we know). The world is the classroom for your spiritual lessons. It's your school for life. The only way you can flunk out is by not showing up. If you drop out, you are destined to the failure of shallow and meaningless living, a.k.a. boredom.

Spirituality cannot and must not be detached from the world.

A spiritual person is someone who does know what is happening in the world. A spiritual person not only reads the daily newspaper, but is actively involved in trying to make the world a better place.

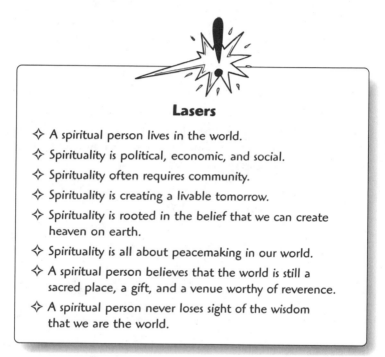

Lasers

✧ A spiritual person lives in the world.

✧ Spirituality is political, economic, and social.

✧ Spirituality often requires community.

✧ Spirituality is creating a livable tomorrow.

✧ Spirituality is rooted in the belief that we can create heaven on earth.

✧ Spirituality is all about peacemaking in our world.

✧ A spiritual person believes that the world is still a sacred place, a gift, and a venue worthy of reverence.

✧ A spiritual person never loses sight of the wisdom that we are the world.

Many of you think of spirituality as being off on a cloud somewhere, as a means of transcending this Earth and all its glaring problems.

Nothing could be farther from the truth. The truly spiritual person is someone who is enmeshed in the pain and problems of our world, as well as being able to celebrate the joy and justice that can still be found in abundance. A spiritual person does not transcend, but descends.

You have to get your hands dirty, your heart broken, and your mind blown away. You must love the world with the kind of love that makes it clear that you are in it for the long haul and that you will always be there. You must passionately care about the creation of the world and all its God-given resources. You must care deeply about all the different races and religions. You must see the whole planet as home and your self as a citizen of the globe.

If you realize that the world is an event of God's grace, then you will be gracious in your treatment of it. Embrace this world with grace—that is our primary spiritual job!

The following is a list of suggested activities for developing a love for the world in which you live and, hopefully, for impacting the kind of person you will *be:*

1. Attend religious services of a religion other than your own, or read about other religions.

2. Interview someone who is a devout member of an Eastern religion, such as Buddhism or Hinduism.

3. Interview someone who is a socialist.

4. Interview someone who is a communist.

5. Interview someone who is involved in an environmental issue.

6. Get involved in helping to solve an environmental issue.

7. Write to your congressperson about an environmental issue.

8. Choose a world problem and learn all you can about it.

9. Try to do something practical to address the problem, and gather some of your friends or family to do the same.

10. Visit a jail or prison—speak with an inmate.

11. Visit a homeless shelter—speak with a guest.

12. Visit a nursing home—speak to a resident.

13. Interview someone with cancer.

14. Interview someone who is paralyzed.

15. Interview someone who is caring for an Alzheimer's patient.

16. Attend a rally.

17. Attend a conference or workshop on social activism.

18. Attend a political convention.

19. Get involved in a political campaign.

20. Attend a religious convention.

21. Interview a lobbyist.

22. Write a letter to the editor.

23. Write an essay on an issue that matters to you.

24. Fight for a piece of legislation.

25. File a petition on a cause or issue that you care deeply about.

26. Participate in the politics of a church or synagogue, or a community of concerned citizens.

27. Find out what the issues are at your school; address them, speak out on them, and take action.

A spiritual person must be a social activist. This is the nature of spirituality. Spirituality is not just trying to transform the soul, but also to change the world. If you are to mature spiritually, you must be willing to get more involved in this world. You must learn how to love this world extravagantly and with abundant forgiveness. For all its craziness, this world is still Miracle Headquarters.

Getting in Touch with Your God

Once during a children's sermon in worship, a small child blurted out the following inquiry: "If I go in my backyard, and I start digging, and I go way down, like to China ... through China ... will I get to heaven and God?" His parents were sitting crimson-faced in their pew, shaking their heads back and forth as a clue to me to say, "Absolutely not!" A vision of their Brian beginning to dig right after church was dancing in their heads. What I did tell Brian was the truth—that I wasn't sure, but that I really, really doubted it.

To be honest, I don't think it is all that hard to get to God because God is always coming to us. Sometimes I feel like God is stalking me—I really do. Now, admittedly, I have been working on this spiritual gig for over 30 years, so I do have a head start on you, but I am always surprised by how often I actually sense God chasing me. I don't think that you have to go or dig or look all that far. I think that God is right under your nose, right at your side. God is your shadow.

Once again, I think you need to stop, look, and listen. The spiritual fact is that God can only be received. You have to open your mind and heart to God. You have to open your whole being to God. God is always in communication with you, and that conversation is literally endless. Sometimes God is tickling you with a lovely memory, poking you in the conscience, or trying to pry you loose with a kick in the proverbial guts.

God is incessantly waving his arms, trying to flag you down to get your attention and to get you to pull over and stop. Only it isn't God who needs the help—it's you. You are the one with the spiritual flat tire, the overheated engine, or the "E" lighting up on your gas gauge for "Empty."

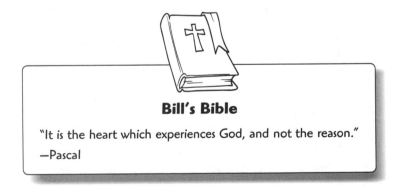

Bill's Bible

"It is the heart which experiences God, and not the reason."
—Pascal

One surefire way to be in touch with God is to turn your senses over to God as you understand Him. Ask God what He sees, hears, smells, tastes, and thinks. Try to experience the world with God's heart. I know this sounds strange, but try it—it really works. You have more of God in you than you know. You are more able to act as if you actually were God than you believe. Obviously, this is a different kind of God-playing. This is putting on God like a cloak or mask, with full recognition that you are not God.

Bill's Bible

"Since God chose you to be the holy people whom he loves, you must *clothe* yourselves with tenderhearted mercy, kindness, gentleness, and patience. You must make allowance for each other's faults and forgive the person who offends you. Remember, the Lord forgave you, so you must forgive others. And the most important piece of clothing you must wear is love. Love is what binds us all together in perfect harmony."

—Colossians 3:12–14

Clothing yourself in God is freeing yourself to think, feel, and experience life, others, and your self as you believe God would. Is it all that hard to do? Not really. It is like when you were a little kid and you would jump off the front steps into your dad's arms. You just have to trust God to catch you. Then jump. That is what is called a leap of faith.

In the Dark

Most spiritual disciplines at first will sound silly to try. Do them anyway. The results will be anything but silly—and you would be really silly not to even try.

Read the following passage of Scripture, and reflect on what it has to say to you about trust, about letting go and trusting God:

> So I tell you, don't worry about everyday life—whether you have enough food, drink, and clothes. Doesn't life consist of more than food and clothing? Look at the birds. They don't need to plant or harvest or put food in barns because your heavenly Father feeds them. And you are far more valuable to him than they are. Can all your worries add a single moment to your life? Of course not.
>
> And why worry about your clothes? Look at the lilies and how they grow. They don't work or make their clothing, yet Solomon in all his glory was not dressed as beautifully as they are. And if God cares so wonderfully for flowers that are here today and gone tomorrow, won't he more surely care for you? You have so little faith!
>
> So don't worry about having enough food or drink or clothing. Why be like the pagans who are so deeply concerned about these things? Your heavenly Father already knows all your needs, and he will give you all you need from day to day if you live for him and make the Kingdom your primary concern.

So don't worry about tomorrow, for tomorrow will bring its own worries. Today's trouble is enough for today.

—Matthew 6:25–34

A great deal is contained in that passage. It is a real challenge to trust God. Still, I know that a good many of you are struggling mightily with the whole *notion* of God. You are not sure what or if you believe. All I ask is that you give yourself permission to use the concept of God. Let yourself define what God means to you. The concept is still vital to spiritual growth, however you define it or understand it. The concept is the primary catalyst for spiritual maturation.

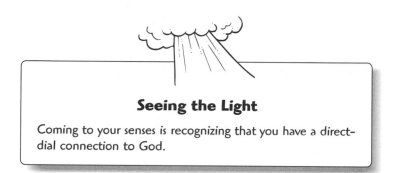

Seeing the Light

Coming to your senses is recognizing that you have a direct-dial connection to God.

Your soul forces you to be in touch with your neighbor. To possess the spiritual strength needed to love and forgive your neighbor, you will be forced to be in touch with God. The force of being in touch with God will transform your whole life. Your life will feel brand new.

The Least You Need to Know

✧ Just like a baby that doesn't receive loving, human contact, your soul will die if it is not touched.

✧ Spirituality is a force—a force that puts you in touch with your soul.

✧ To possess the spiritual strength needed to love and forgive your neighbor, you will be forced to be in touch with God.

✧ The force of being in touch with God will transform your whole life. Your life will feel brand new.

Developing Good Taste

In This Chapter

✧ Why taste is another powerful spiritual metaphor

✧ How you can become a spiritual gourmet by developing a discriminating palate

✧ Why learning how to get just the right mix of flavors—and how not to overstuff the soul—is a vital skill to learn to enjoy the whole experience of life

✧ How to choose a well-balanced spiritual diet

✧ Why bittersweet is life's most common flavor—and one that you need to acquire a taste for

Spiritual good taste has zip to do with fashion or breeding. Good taste is a potent metaphor for spirituality. Spiritually speaking, good taste is as simple as knowing what tastes good, which is to know what *is* good. From a spiritual perspective, good taste is all about being able to recognize when something or someone is worthy of ingesting and good for the spiritual diet. In this chapter, you will learn how to be a "spiritual gourmet" at the table of life.

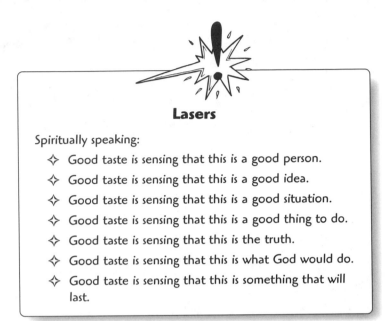

Lasers

Spiritually speaking:

✧ Good taste is sensing that this is a good person.

✧ Good taste is sensing that this is a good idea.

✧ Good taste is sensing that this is a good situation.

✧ Good taste is sensing that this is a good thing to do.

✧ Good taste is sensing that this is the truth.

✧ Good taste is sensing that this is what God would do.

✧ Good taste is sensing that this is something that will last.

A Spiritual Gourmet

A gourmet is someone who knows a lot about good food. A gourmet knows whether all the ingredients are fresh, whether the recipe has been followed, and whether the meal has been prepared with passion. A gourmet enjoys the whole experience of dining. From the flowers on the table, to the wine with each course, a gourmet revels in the meal as a whole. A gourmet savors the taste of each and every dish, each and every flavor. A gourmet has a discriminating palate.

Now, let me translate this into spiritual language. To be a spiritual gourmet, you have these characteristics:

✧ Are meant to know a lot about the art of spirituality

✧ Need to know if something you are doing is of real value

✧ Should know if a person you meet is the real thing

✧ Are meant to be someone with significant insight and depth

✦ Are meant to be aware of your own callings

✦ Should possess a good eye for truth and falsehood

✦ Are to be a fine friend

✦ Are to be conscious of your whole world

A spiritual gourmet is an individual who makes excellent choices. Just as a food gourmet knows how to put together a wonderful menu, a spiritual gourmet knows how to put together a wonderful life. In the same way that a food gourmet knows how to choose just the right ingredients to create the perfect flavor, a spiritual gourmet knows how to create a life that has just enough fun, just enough service, just enough sacrifice, just enough work, and more than enough love.

Seeing the Light

Coming to your senses means to become a spiritual gourmet. A spiritual gourmet possesses a discriminating soul that is wise enough to sense what is genuinely good, and a willingness to savor that goodness.

A spiritual gourmet understands that spirituality is an art that involves the whole person—body, mind, heart, and soul. Physically, emotionally, and spiritually, a spiritual gourmet is a connoisseur of the best that life has to offer, gives only his or her best, and brings out the best in others. These people make the whole world a better place in which to live.

Too Much ... Not Enough

A gourmet cook will know immediately whether something tastes too bland, or salty, or excessively sweet. A gourmet will know whether something has been cooked too long or not enough. A gourmet can tell by sight, texture, and even aroma whether a food has been prepared correctly. Everything about a fine meal sends signals, and the gourmet has mastered the art of picking up those signals.

Seeing the Light

Coming to your senses means knowing when the soul is being underfed or overfed, or when life has no spice or is too spicy to digest.

If you are to become a spiritual gourmet, you will need to know whether your life is spiced and prepared properly. Is there enough time in your life for recreation? To be alone with your self and God? To restore your emotional and spiritual balance? Does your life contain enough meaningful activity to make it feel worthwhile? Is your life being true to your callings? Are you using your talents? Are you sharing your gifts?

In our culture, we tend to deal with time as an enemy. We buy time, kill time, spend time. Like a gourmet chef who will take all the time necessary to make sure that the meal is just right, a spiritual gourmet is also comfortable with taking all the time the soul requires. Spiritual gourmets make time work for them. They are not slaves to the clock. They obey only the messages of the heart.

Just a Taste

Gourmet food is never served in heaping helpings. Gourmet dining is never a plate that is completely covered with food.

A gourmet meal is many tastes. The portions are small but ample enough to leave one satisfied. The goal is not to feel overwhelmed by a taste, or to leave the table bloated.

A spiritual gourmet is also sensitive to not trying to stuff the soul. Yes, the soul can be overwhelmed. Your soul can be bloated to the point of bursting. How? By literally trying to think too much, by dwelling on a feeling, or by becoming obsessive about certain behaviors, even prayer and worship. A spiritual gourmet knows how to put before the soul a plate that offers just enough food, with more than enough flavor.

In the Dark

When your senses are overwhelmed, they will shut down. Spiritual shut-down is the equivalent of living in a cocoon or being in a coma.

Spoiled Means Rotten

The ecumenical youth group had just finished a fierce game of Frisbee football. Several of the guys and girls raced ahead to get to the beverages in the church refrigerator. I took my time. I'm old and chubby. When I walked into the church I could hear people screaming and gagging. I was confused. I walked into the kitchen to see that these kids had gotten hold of some bad orange juice and a carton of spoiled milk.

The taste of anything spoiled is rotten—it is enough to make you gag. It takes a long time to get the taste out of your mouth. Spiritually speaking, a soul that is spoiled is also rotten. Being around those who expect the world to wait on them is enough to make you gag. If a child has been spoiled by his or her parents, it will take a long, long time to undo the spiritual damage. A spoiled soul is simply not capable of seeing or hearing or being touched by God. God cannot penetrate the thick layer of conceit that coats the spoiled soul.

Seeing the Light

Coming to your senses means throwing out everything that might spoil your soul. A spoiled soul is a soul that has gone sour on life. A spiritual gourmet would never serve the soul anything spoiled. Spoiled always means rotten.

An Acquired Taste

A gourmet has learned to savor. A gourmet takes ample time to notice a flavor or to distinguish an aroma. A gourmet has learned how to use his or her taste buds to the max of their ability. A gourmet has acquired a skill in tasting. A gourmet has acquired a taste for everything, or at least the capacity to recognize it for what it is. A gourmet has acquired a taste that he or she already possessed: The taste buds are God-given. They simply needed training.

To be a spiritual gourmet is also an acquired taste. A spiritual gourmet has acquired a taste for a wide variety of emotional and spiritual experiences. A spiritual gourmet can savor the experiences of solitude, stillness, and silence. A spiritual gourmet seeks to maximize the powers of the soul and trains the soul to savor and enjoy all those experiences that can yield satisfaction, maturity, and joy.

Seeing the Light

Coming to your senses means acquiring a taste for a wide range of human experience and enjoying the rich diversity of the banquet set before you.

Soul Food

The soul must be nourished. Just like the body, the soul must be replenished on a daily basis. If the soul is not fed, you can feel your spirit getting weary.

Many of you take excellent care of your bodies. You do rigorous exercise. You work out regularly. You try to eat right by eating lots of fruits and veggies and drinking lots of water.

But few of you take good care of your souls. The soul tends to be underfed to the point of starving. The starving soul lacks energy (no spirit), muscle tone (no convictions), and motivation (no use). A starving soul is just skin and bones. There's no muscle, flesh, or even fat. The soul has no capacity to do its work, and no will to get up and look alive.

How do you nourish the soul? Well, we have already covered some of the answers, but it will be good to review:

✧ The soul is nourished by taking time to do nothing.

✧ The soul is nourished by having time to play.

✧ The soul needs to be fed by the imagination and intuition.

✧ The soul needs three square meals a day: silence, solitude, and stillness.

✧ The soul needs a daily vitamin of humor and humility.

✧ The soul must be flushed out with forgiveness.

✧ The soul needs time to chase beauty.

✧ The soul needs to listen to the echoes of the Earth.

✧ The soul needs to have prayer and worship in its diet.

✧ The soul needs an occasional sweet of pure pleasure.

✧ The soul needs to be exercised with acts of kindness and mercy; service and sacrifice; and love and hope.

✧ The soul needs a faith workout at least a couple times a week. A faith workout should consist of several repetitions of life's most engaging questions, a counting of blessings, a claiming of wrongs, a request for forgiveness, and a commitment to love.

Seeing the Light

Coming to your senses means learning how to nourish the soul and making sure that you never allow the soul to starve.

A Well-Balanced Diet

In the New Testament, numerous stories tell of Jesus going off by himself to the mountains or desert to pray. He would withdraw from the chaos and demands of the world and his life, and find a time of rest and spiritual refreshment. This is a powerful image because, for those of you who are Christian, it means that even God knew how to take a break. For those of you who are not Christian, it still means that an ancient book of wisdom, the Bible, also advocates the taking of time for soul restoration.

Most of you have lives that are woefully out of balance. You are busy beyond belief. You often complain about not having enough time to breathe—which is saying something pretty powerful. You keep your friends happy. You try to keep parents and teachers happy. You just have no time for your self—and for God.

A well-balanced spiritual diet is one that takes ample time to rest, relax, and renew. A spiritual diet is one that recognizes that you are not meant to conquer the world, to keep everyone happy, or to do it all. A spiritual diet has a daily dose of humility, a recognition that you are a human, and that human beings require time for doing nothing. You need time for prayer and reflection, time for worship and praise, time for healing, and time for relocating hope.

Seeing the Light

Coming to your senses means keeping your self in balance. A well-balanced spiritual diet features a good deal of time spent relaxing and restoring the soul. A soul out of balance is a soul that is whipped by too much work, a slave to success.

In Bad Taste

It was a hot night in May. This summer-type heat wave was predicted to last all week. Many of the members of the ecumenical youth group were complaining bitterly about the possibility of having to be trapped in school during this heat wave. I had to admit, I remember how hard it was to concentrate and study after that first hint of summer had arrived.

Our discussion that night was on jealousy, and to be honest, it was going nowhere. The kids' minds were elsewhere, and most just did not feel like talking about anything heavy or serious. It was a combination of spring fever and a topic they were just not interested in. The sound of thunder and the sight of lightning broke any focus the group had, and I surrendered to the realization that tonight's discussion was a bomb.

Bill's Bible

"Life is a banquet, but most poor fools are starving to death."

—Auntie Mame

On a whim, I said "Let's go to Goat Hill." The whole group looked at me with a collective face that said "Why on earth would we want to do that?" By this time the rain and wind was torrential. I said "So we can go mudsliding!" Though they were still not sure what I had in mind, it sounded crazy, and that was good enough for them.

We had a ball. The hill was like a river, and it was no trouble at all to go sliding down it a good 50 yards or more. After an hour of mudsliding, we were a mess. We were all wall-to-wall mud. The laughing was nonstop, as was the mud-slinging. The youth night was a memorable success.

Now, admittedly, a few parents thought my decision was in professional bad taste. They complained of the muddy mess and the potential for catching a cold. One mother sent me a laundry bill. I gladly paid it. It had been worth it.

Sometimes you have to do something crazy. You have to break out of a mold or a rut. My grandmother always said that the only difference between a rut and a grave was the depth. That insight has proved true in my life. You need to shake things up once in a while.

There will always be those who condemn you for taking a risk or doing something that the world might say is in bad taste, but then again, the world probably thought that the three wise men were complete idiots for choosing to follow a star in the sky. If you never risk doing something in bad taste, you will have a very limited repertoire of experience and a very limited life.

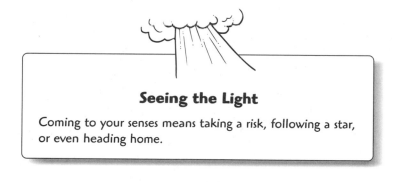

Seeing the Light

Coming to your senses means taking a risk, following a star, or even heading home.

Bittersweet

I want to share an anecdote with you. It is quite recent and quite private. I share it with you because it is truly the best illustration I can think of for the bittersweet taste of so much of life. Bittersweet is life's most common flavor, and it is a taste that you are beginning to know. This is a taste that you will know intimately if you choose to mature spiritually. In life, the bitter and the sweet go hand in hand—they have been married for years and years. You might even refer to them as a lovely old couple.

Here is a bittersweet story.

My father has Alzheimer's disease, which is a fancy name for a mind that has become Swiss cheese, a progressive disease where nothing can fill the ever-increasing number of holes. My father has lost me down one of those holes and has not recognized me for the past two years. That is a bitterly painful

129

experience, seeing and touching, even hearing, a man you know so well, but who now looks at you as if you were the newspaper boy. He is friendly, but he can't remember your name. He says hello, but not much else.

When I return to Racine, Wisconsin, my beloved hometown, I visit Dad with my mother. My mother remains devoted to him, and it is a bitter pill for her to swallow that he no longer recognizes his son. She always tries to act as if he still knows who I am, on some level. She almost tries to will it to be so.

On this particular evening, Dad was sitting alone at a table, with a full plate of food in front of him. Mom had brought along some of her own special mashed potatoes and a Jell-O salad that he had always loved. We fed him Mom's food first. I watched Mom gently feeding him, much as I remembered her feeding my son Justin as an infant. She was talking with him all the time, filling him in on all the news about his wise son who had arrived from the East.

Seeing the Light

Remember, the religious establishment thought that most of what Jesus did and said was in bad taste.

What Mom failed to notice as she fed Dad (her own eyes are badly diseased with a condition called wet macular degeneration) was that he was not swallowing. Finally, I informed her that Dad was beginning to look like a chipmunk, and Mom giggled and put down the fork. She told me that we had other people to feed that night, and we would get back to Dad. I said fine and proceeded to feed my assigned patient. Suddenly I heard Mom scream "Oh my God, he is eating the flowers." Having left my father unattended while we fed a few other residents, my father was indeed now chowing down on the daisies that had once prettily adorned the table.

My mother and I looked at each other in horror, and then burst out laughing. Mom said "Oh well, hell, maybe it's some good protein." We laughed and laughed. We laughed until the tears flowed. We laughed until my mom had to scurry to the bathroom.

I know. You probably think my mother and I are warped or have a pretty sick sense of humor. That may be so, but not in this case. In this case, we were simply choosing to see the sweetness contained in the bitter. We were able to laugh and love in spite of the absurdity of contending with my Dad's Alzheimer's disease.

We could have been furious. We could have filed a report with the state against the nursing home. We could have left the nursing home in tears. Well, we did, but it was with the sweet tears of laughter.

Life is Good Friday and Easter Sunday. It is saying hello and saying goodbye. It is tears of sorrow and tears of joy. It is babies and caskets. It is good health and bad health. It is emotional peaks and valleys. It is lovely weather and tornadoes and blizzards. It is weddings and anniversaries, as well as divorces and visitation rights. It is crisis and calm. Life is bittersweet—you have to become familiar with that taste if you are going to spiritually mature.

Seeing the Light

Coming to your senses is learning that much of life is bittersweet. Spirituality is about acquiring a taste for the bittersweet.

As we move on in this book, I plan to introduce you to a good chunk of Scripture. I do so for a few reasons: First, I know that some of you have an aversion to the Bible, and I hope that you can get over it. Second, I want you to see how much practical wisdom the Bible contains. Third, and finally, I hope that you will be able to see that the Bible still has something to say to your life and your world.

The following piece of Scripture I find amazing. What is truly amazing to me is that these words are in the Bible. They are so honest. They are so real. They are so bittersweet. Ecclesiastes, the preacher, is telling it like it is:

> For everything there is a season, and a time for every matter under heaven: a time to be born, and a time to die; a time to plant, and a time to pluck up what is planted; a time to kill, and a time to heal; a time to break down, and a time to build up; a time to weep, and a time to laugh; a time to mourn, and a time to dance; a time to cast away stones, and a time to gather stones together; a time to embrace, and a time to refrain from embracing; a time to seek, and a time to lose; a time to keep, and a time to cast away; a time to rend, and a time to sew; a time to keep silence, and a time to speak; a time to love, and a time to hate; a time for war, and a time for peace. What gain has the worker from his toil? I have thought about this in connection with the various kinds of work God has given people to do. God has made everything beautiful for its own time. He has planted eternity in the human heart, but even so, people cannot see the whole scope of God's work from beginning to end.
>
> —Ecclesiastes 3:1–11

Ecclesiastes is correct. You cannot fully comprehend the will and wisdom of God. Much of your life will remain shrouded in mystery. This is why you must learn to enjoy the taste of bittersweet, for although you will get a sweet taste of eternity from time to time, you will also know the bitterness of your limited time and experience. Accepting our limitations, when they are God-given, forms the foundation upon which you will build your entire spiritual life.

The Least You Need to Know

✧ You must become a spiritual gourmet in order to discern and enjoy all the tastes life has to offer.

✧ A spiritual gourmet knows just what spices to add to life for just the right balance of flavor.

✧ A spiritual gourmet is nourished by "soul food."

✧ A spiritual gourmet instinctually chooses a well-balanced diet and never overwhelms or stuffs the soul.

✧ Sometimes you have to take the risk of bad taste. If you never risk doing something in bad taste, you will limit your experience and thus your life.

✧ Bittersweet is life's most common flavor—you need to acquire a taste for it.

Part 3

Being Spiritual

You live in a culture of doers. America is addicted to doing. You are taught to measure yourself by what you do for a living. When you ask people how they are, they seldom tell you, but instead tell you what they are doing. Doing = value and worth. To be somebody special = somebody who does a lot. Our culture worships the person who can keep 20 balls juggling in the air. If you have a sour stomach from stress it is only a sign of your success. Doing nothing is a sign of laziness—it is the business of losers.

Spirituality is not about doing. Spirituality is about being. *It is not that spirituality condemns your work or your busy-ness; it doesn't. Spirituality will, however, give balance and perspective to your doing. Spirituality will keep what you are doing in focus. Spirituality will strive to focus your doing on those things in Life which truly matter.*

Chapter 9

Be Real

In This Chapter

- ✧ Why being honest with yourself is the only way to be the real you

- ✧ Why avoiding the bogus is vital

- ✧ How to be the same person on the outside as you are on the inside.

- ✧ How being centered will help you to ride out the storms in your life

- ✧ Why coming clean is the only way to let the real you shine through

As I said at the very beginning, I like adolescents. I admire many adolescents. I especially admire your seemingly innate ability to distinguish the genuine from the phony.

I pay close attention to the things you say, especially the small cryptic phrases that periodically dominate your dialogue: "Get a life"; "Lighten up"; "Word up." Recently, the catch-all word used by a bulk of my youth is "bogus."

Bogus. Again, I think your choices of words and phrases are revelatory. In this case, I believe you are calling attention to how many things in your world seem phony, artificial, and untrustworthy. Can you trust a politician or preacher to tell you the truth? Can you trust that what you are buying is honestly what you thought you were getting? Can you trust that your parents' marriage is real love? Can you trust anything to be the real thing, or to last, or to fulfill what has been promised?

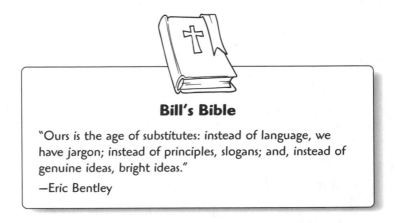

Bill's Bible

"Ours is the age of substitutes: instead of language, we have jargon; instead of principles, slogans; and, instead of genuine ideas, bright ideas."

—Eric Bentley

The Coca Cola company spent thousands of dollars to try to find the one word that rang true for the American teen; the one word that held real appeal for an adolescent. The word was *real*. Coke became the "real thing." In one of the great ironies of our culture, a soft drink that has nothing to do with anything real is advertised as the source of all that is real. How sad is that? It's sad, but we do indeed buy it— literally.

Bogus

Bogus means "artificial." It is a word that tells us something is phony. Bogus means that whatever it is, it isn't genuine.

Think about how it feels to watch a friend being shown attention and affection only because he or she has a car or concert tickets to offer. Think about how it feels to see someone flirting, when you know that the flirtation means nothing to the person doing the flirting, but everything to the person who is the object of the flirtation. Think about how it feels to watch a parent trying to act like a teenager. Think about how it feels to witness a teacher acting like a peer or a pal. Think about how it feels to hear the words "I love you" when you know down deep that there is not an ounce of truth in the declaration.

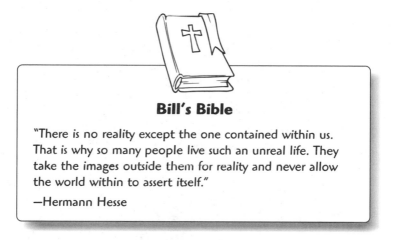

Bill's Bible

"There is no reality except the one contained within us. That is why so many people live such an unreal life. They take the images outside them for reality and never allow the world within to assert itself."

—Hermann Hesse

It feels sickening. It makes you queasy. It makes you want to squirm. Phoniness, superficiality, being bogus—it's all nauseating behavior. Yet you do it. I do it. To some extent, we all do it. But why?

✦ You do it to fit in, or to belong.

✦ You do it because it is easier than being genuine.

✦ You do it to be popular.

✦ You do it to impress someone.

✦ You may do it to get even.

✦ You may do it because it makes you feel powerful.

✦ You may do it because everyone else does it.

✧ You may do it because you have forgotten what it feels like to be really honest.

✧ You may do it without even knowing that you are doing it—it has become a habit.

Being bogus is an easy habit to develop. Lying to yourself and to others works like dominoes: Once one lie goes down, all kinds of lies are quick to follow. You may not think of being phony as actual lying, but it is. Even if we all do it, a lie is a lie. The real danger is that you might someday find yourself living a lie. Let me explain.

You get up late. The alarm clock wasn't set. You burn the toast. Your ride to school has left without you. You run to school, and you are sweating like a big-time wrestler. You go to your first class and realize that you have forgotten your homework. You get a test back at the end of class and learn that you flunked. On the way to the next class, someone asks you how you are, and you smile and say, "Great, how about you?"

In the Dark

Little white lies often turn into big black stains on the soul.

No big deal. Right? In some ways, it is no big deal. On another level, a spiritual plane, it is a very big deal. This kind of lying is the way you learn to detach. You detach from what you honestly feel, think, believe, and even experience. It becomes more important to create a got-it-together image than it is to be true to your real self. The image makes you feel safe and secure. The image makes you feel in control and in charge.

As you invest more trust in the image, the image more often becomes the reality you present. The farther the image moves away from the real you, the more dangerous the whole enterprise becomes. Most of the anxiety and stress that you feel in your life is the direct result of the tension between your image and the real you. The more distant the image is from the truth of who you are, the more you are at risk for having some major emotional, relational, even physical problems.

In the Dark

The trouble with a good image is that images cannot reflect genuine goodness.

Congruence

Congruence is a term found in geometry. Congruent triangles coincide at all points when superimposed upon each other. This is the state of being in agreement, the state of corresponding.

In spiritual language, to be a congruent person is to be someone who shows on the outside exactly what is being experienced on the inside. Congruent people are those who do the following:

✧ Do not try to hide their humanness

✧ Honestly claim their feelings, and will show them

✧ Honestly claim their thoughts, and will speak them

✧ Honestly claim their beliefs, and will live them

✧ Honestly claim their mistakes, and will try to correct them

✧ Honestly claim their failures, and will try to learn from them

✧ Honestly claim their doubts and questions, and will raise them

✧ Do not pretend to be anyone else

✧ Do not wear masks or attempt to fool anyone

✧ Try to be rigorously honest at all times, unless there is a chance of doing someone unnecessary harm

✧ Are conscious of being honest with God

✧ Are aware of who they really are, and strive to reveal that soul

A congruent person is the real thing. What you see is what you get. A congruent person wants to be known, understood, and loved, and that can't happen if what you present to the world is an artificial image. You can't love an image—at least, not for very long.

Here is a good test of your own personal congruence:

1. How do you let people know when you are sad?
2. How do you let people know that you are angry?
3. What do you do with your fears?
4. How is your image different than the real you?
5. Who knows you best? How and why?
6. How hard does someone have to work to get to know the real you? How and why?
7. When do you feel a need to be phony or act artificial?
8. Is it hard to maintain your image?
9. Has your image gotten you into trouble? Out of trouble?
10. How often do you lie?
11. What do you tend to lie about?
12. What emotions do you struggle to express?

13. What beliefs do you find tough to share?

14. Who do you know who seems to live a lie?

15. What lies do your parents live?

16. What lies do your friends live?

17. What is the biggest lie you have ever told?

18. What price have you paid for lying?

19. What do you still have a tough time admitting?

20. What do you need to honestly address?

Staying Centered

Hurricanes are huge storms. They can be miles wide. At the perimeter, a hurricane has ferocious winds and torrential rains—how much wind and how much rain depends on the rank of the hurricane. I have experienced one Category 2 storm, one Category 3 storm, and one between Categories 3 and 4. Hurricanes are eerie and frightening monsters to watch lumber up the Eastern seaboard, and they're haunting to experience firsthand. At the center of every hurricane is what is referred to as the eye of the storm. The eye is calm. The eye is often sun-drenched and brings blue skies. The eye becomes a completely other world encased in a storm shell. The eye is a patch of pure peace, surrounded by warring winds.

The soul is like the eye of a hurricane. The soul is a place of calm. The soul is your center. It is the core of the real you. At your center is the you that is God-given. At your core is a you that knows that you are unique. The soul informs you, when given the chance, that your greatest fear is realizing how wonderful you are. There is a quiet at your core, at the very center of who you really are, that shouts of your unlimited potential to be all that you ever dreamed you could be.

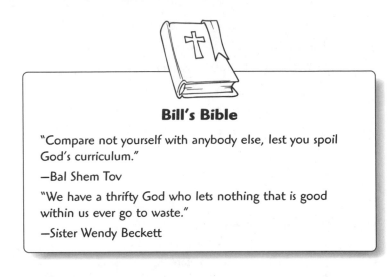

Bill's Bible

"Compare not yourself with anybody else, lest you spoil God's curriculum."

—Bal Shem Tov

"We have a thrifty God who lets nothing that is good within us ever go to waste."

—Sister Wendy Beckett

The soul is likewise surrounded by fierce winds. These are the winds of worry and stress, the frenzied pursuit of success, and the chaotic efforts to always maintain just the right image. Daily the soul does battle with winds that can damage and destroy your spirit. The soul is always in danger of being flooded by the demands of the world, the pressure cooker of trying to keep everyone happy, and the storm surge that is the relentless pursuit of perfection—trying to play God.

The soul, like the eye, cannot exist without the storm of life. The soul must do battle with the winds and rain. The soul must embrace the reality of the storm, yet know that the eye is every bit as real. Whenever you are doing battle with the pressures and pains and problems of being a human being, remember that you have within you a safe, calm harbor. Go there and give yourself rest. Ride out the storm. To be centered is to free the soul to announce this to the world:

✧ I am unique.

✧ I am called to accomplish significant things.

✧ I am empowered to make a difference.

✧ I am worthy of respect and love.

✧ I am worthy of God's pride.

✧ I possess great goodness.

✧ I am a co-creator with God.

✧ I can become my dreams.

✧ I possess greater courage than I even know.

✧ Let me show you who I really am.

✧ Let me show you who I really can be.

✧ Let me show you the divine spark that fires me, the spark that ignites the real me.

Coming Clean

The real you is pure. The real you is spotless. The real you is forever fresh. The real you is blessed. The real you contains the seed of God.

The real you is often plastered with makeup, covered by the mask of image or reputation. The real you is often coated with the grime of just being alive.

Far too often, you feel that you must change the way you appear in order to please someone. You change your look, your outfit, your attitude, and even your beliefs. You try to pour your self into someone else's mold, but it never works. You only make a mess of things. Down deep, you are sickened by playing this game, by trying to be someone that you know you're not.

Coming clean means letting the soul take a good long soak in a bath of grace, the unconditional love and forgiveness of God. Coming clean is trusting God to remove the soil and the stain. All you need is to crawl in the tub and soak. But where do you find this tub? Where do you take this bath?

Remember, the soul can be bathed in the following:

✧ Silence	✧ Community
✧ Solitude	✧ Remembrance
✧ Stillness	✧ Worship
✧ Beauty	✧ Friendship
✧ Prayer	✧ Family
✧ Gratitude	✧ Love
✧ Service	

The Genuine Article

Have you ever watched *Antiques Roadshow* on TV? Okay, I know that it isn't in your top 10. This is a show with a simple premise. Antique experts travel to a city and set up shop. People from all over the city come to have their supposed antiques evaluated. These folks bring every kind of antique or collectible imaginable.

What gives me a kick out of the show is the look on the faces of those people who have brought in an antique fake, as well as those individuals who discover that their antique is the genuine article and is worth a small fortune. The fun is in realizing that it is so hard to tell whether something is a fake. Only the experts can explain the difference.

When it comes to being the real you, you are the expert. You may have a parent, teacher, or friend who is well-educated on the subject of the real you, but you alone are the expert. Only you know whether you are being true to your real self—you and God. But, if an expert stops doing his or her job, ceases to evaluate for authenticity, and doesn't keep up with the science of self-evaluation, that person will quickly find that he or she lacks the knowledge and skill to do the job.

If you don't take time to evaluate your own attitudes and activities, and take time to scrutinize the image you present to the world, you will lose track of the real you. As the Bible says, you can sell your soul. The most common way to sell your soul is to simply misplace it. You lose track of your soul by being preoccupied with the demands of keeping up the image.

Take this brief reality check and see how you are doing today:

Reality Check

Complete these sentences.

1. Today, I have been feeling ....

2. Today, I have been thinking about ....

3. Today, my attitude has been ....

4. Today, I have been worrying about ....

5. Today, I have been really happy about ....

6. Today, I have been acting ....

7. Today, I have been honest with myself about ....

8. Today, I have not been honest with myself about ....

9. Today, I have pretended to be ....

10. Today, I have been true to ....

Honest to Goodness

Let me challenge you today to be true to your self. Be the real you. Be rigorously honest with your self. Do your best to show others the authentic you. Do your best to show God the genuine article. Do the work of peeling away the layers of makeup, masks, and image to get to the real you. Get to the Tootsie Roll center in your Tootsie Pop—get through all that candy coating.

Don't put on an act. It is exhausting to live life on stage. It is spiritually draining to live life as a performance—no matter how good you are in the role. You still have to live with the real you and your real feelings and thoughts. There is no way to ultimately escape that reality—you are stuck with you.

In the Dark

If your life is all just an act, when the curtain comes down and the show has closed, where will you go? What will you do?

However, rather than think of it as being stuck, why not choose to enjoy the intimacy of the relationship? Get to know your self. Be a good friend to yourself. Choose to treat yourself kindly and with compassion. Be generous in praise. Be quick to forgive. Be patient. Love who you are.

There is a parable—a tiny story with a huge point—in the Bible about a man who travels a dangerous road to Jericho and winds up getting robbed, beaten, and left for dead. All the poor man can do is wait to see if anyone will come to help. A priest walks by. A Levite walks by. Both men are powerful fixtures in the religious establishment, yet they show complete indifference to the battered guy at the side of the road. Finally, a Samaritan, a race of people despised by the religious establishment of that time, comes to the man's rescue.

The Good Samaritan kneels and touches the man. He applies ointment to his many wounds. He picks up the man and carries him to an inn. He pays the bill at the inn. He tells the innkeeper that he will come back to see that the man has fully recovered, and if there are more bills, he will pay those too. The Samaritan's love is extravagant and unconditional. I think of the Good Samaritan as the world's first bleeding heart liberal—all compassion, all mercy, all love.

Bill's Bible

"What you are is God's gift to you; what you make of it is your gift to God."

—Anthony Dalla Villa

These are the points of the parable: First, the people you often least expect to be of help prove the most helpful. Second, our responsibility to our neighbor is to do whatever it takes.

Third, when we choose to help someone, we are ultimately doing the most good for ourselves.

You are often the person who is least likely to be good to yourself. You are often your own worst critic. You beat yourself up over trivial mistakes. You tend to be unforgiving of your failures. You frequently expect perfection. When you are the one battered and bruised at the side of the road, you tend to also be like the priest or Levite in the story—you just walk on by.

Today, I am asking you to learn how to be your own Good Samaritan. You need to learn to treat yourself as well as the Good Samaritan treated that guy left to die on the side of the road. When you are feeling battered and bruised, you need to kneel down and take care of yourself. You need to know how to apply ointment to your wounds, and how to grant yourself the time and space to heal. You must be willing to pay the price.

Here are some tips on how to take good care of your self and how to serve as your own Good Samaritan.

The Good Samaritan Guide

1. What do you really like about yourself?
2. Of what are you most proud?
3. What accomplishments do you need to celebrate?
4. How do you celebrate yourself?
5. What rewards do you give yourself?
6. When you are really down in the dumps, what do you most often need?
7. When you are wounded, how can someone help to heal the wound?
8. Do you know how to ask for help?
9. Who do you ask for help?

10. Who responds to your requests for assistance?
11. Do you ever ask God for help?
12. How do you help yourself?
13. What makes you feel great?
14. When are you truly relaxed?
15. When was the last time you felt genuinely happy?
16. When and where are you at your best?
17. What needs healing in your heart?
18. How do you show yourself respect?
19. What do you admire in yourself?
20. How do you take care of your soul?

Honest to goodness, honesty does lead to goodness. It forms the circle of the spiritual life. Being honest with yourself and being the real you frees you to love and be loved. That's how the immense goodness within you gets released—and that's the real you.

The Least You Need to Know

✧ Be honest, genuine, and real.

✧ Avoid the bogus.

✧ Be congruent. Be the same person on the outside as you are on the inside.

✧ Be centered. Know that within you is a strong, secure, safe place. Approach life from the center of that abundant confidence.

✧ Come clean. Remove the masks and makeup. Let the real you shine through. Get rid of the grime of phoniness and artificiality.

Chapter 10

Be Alive

In This Chapter

✧ The ways in which you may often unknowingly choose to be spiritually dead

✧ Why you need to be fully awake and fully aware in order to receive the gifts God has for you daily

✧ How to be ready to learn the lessons of each day

✧ The ways in which you must be ready to mature each day allow the day to move you forward in your own spiritual growth

✧ How loving life can be the most difficult, and yet, the most important, way to be open

When I still lived in Wisconsin, I took the high school youth group I led there on a retreat. At the very beginning of it, I asked the youth how it felt to be stoned, wasted, and buzzed. They all laughed. They didn't think I was serious. They didn't think I would ever expect them to give an honest answer.

I asked them to trust me. I told them that their answers would never be repeated. They went quiet and became noticeably reflective. Suddenly a few words and phrases began to be blurted out: "Calm." "Relaxed." "At ease." "Mellow." "At peace with the world." "No worries." "No hassles." "No fears." "On top of the world." "Pretty damn good."

At the close of the retreat, I asked them to use their imaginations and describe how it would feel to die. Admittedly, this is a very tough question. They looked at me puzzled. Again, they could see that I was serious, and was waiting until they formed some answers. They thought about the question for some time.

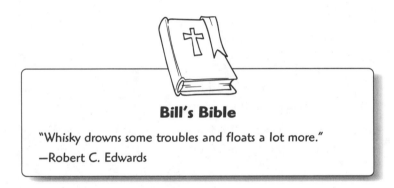

Bill's Bible

"Whisky drowns some troubles and floats a lot more."
—Robert C. Edwards

Again, the answers were blurted out: "Calm." "At ease." "At peace." "No problems or hassles." "No worries or fears." "On top of the world." "Pretty damn good ... I doubt I would ever want to leave."

What the youth group did not know was that I had recorded their earlier answers to the inquiry about how it felt to be stoned, wasted, and buzzed. I played it back to them. It was now almost 48 hours later. They were dumbstruck. They immediately recognized that what they often called "getting high" had been described with the exact same words as life's lowest low—death. It was a very sobering revelation.

In the Dark

To be stoned is to turn the heart to rock. To be wasted is to waste the gift of the moment. To be buzzed is to have reduced your soul to the size of an insect.

Choosing to Be Dead

Don't think anybody can choose to be dead? Think again. It is called deadening, and it is really quite easy to do. Think of it this way. When I talk with adolescents, you often tell me that you just want your life to go smoothly. You are sick of the ups and downs. You are tired of all the rough spots, the problems, and the pains. You just want things to calm down. You would just like a hassle-free day.

Sounds fair. But have you ever seen a flat line on a heart monitor? That is what you are wishing for—a life without any life, to die before you die, and to be deadened to the realities of your physical, emotional, and spiritual worlds.

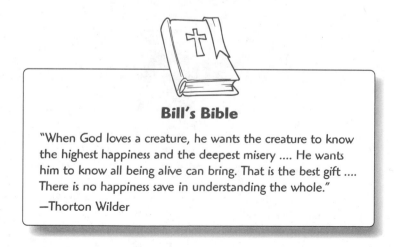

Bill's Bible

"When God loves a creature, he wants the creature to know the highest happiness and the deepest misery .... He wants him to know all being alive can bring. That is the best gift .... There is no happiness save in understanding the whole."
—Thorton Wilder

You may not know it, but there are infinite ways to deaden the soul. Here are some you might frequently use:

✦ Watching TV, even when you are not interested at all

✦ Listening to music to the point that you can no longer hear it

✦ Drinking and drugging

✦ Binge-eating or starving

✦ Engaging in compulsive shopping

✦ Engaging in compulsive sexual activity

✦ Denying your feelings

✦ Spacing out

✦ Being constantly busy

✦ Excessively exercising

✦ Retreating into fantasy games and videos

✦ Using pornography

✦ Playing on the computer

✦ Avoiding intimacy of any kind

✦ Avoiding falling in love

✦ Never sharing honestly with anyone

✦ Using the silent treatment on someone

✦ Lying

✦ Keeping family and or personal secrets

In the Dark

Most secrets that are kept in the dark begin to rot and smell. Secret-keeping is rarely noble; most of the time, it is just plain stupid. It is highly unlikely that you can be healthy and happy while carrying around the stinking garbage of some secret. Secrets can kill the will.

Awake and Aware

Whenever I travel with a youth group for any length of time, there will always be one day ruined because the group is too exhausted to function. No matter how much I plead with the group to get some sleep, I am convinced that it is physically impossible for a group of teenagers to be together and get good rest. There are always the all-night conversations, giggling, farting contests, futile attempts to sneak out, and the ritual of listening to tunes and flirting until dawn. I have screamed, pleaded, yelled, and threatened. I have told the whole group I would take them home. Still, on a week-long trip, at least one day will be destroyed by sleep deprivation.

Bill's Bible

"If I were to begin life again, I should want it as it was. I would only open my eyes a little more."

—Jules Renard

On a recent trip to Milwaukee with my Shelter Island Ecumenical Youth Group, the day we lost was the one day when I really wanted them to see the city's extraordinary art museum. The group was collectively comatose. They were in a stupor. They were crabby. In the car, they were constantly bickering with each other over radio and seat selections. They looked like death warmed over: gray, ghastly, and ghostish.

The visit to the museum was a complete waste of time. They saw little and were even less interested. All over the museum I found my group napping or sitting on the floor inhaling Cokes or coffee. All the modern art I hoped would inspire and challenge them was met with yawns and endless questions of "When are we leaving?" I was furious. I could not believe that

they were missing a golden opportunity to see some unforgettable art. That night they also slept their way through a
Brewers baseball game. My youth group had been dead tired.
They were dead to the world. They were so out of it with
weariness that not one thing could enter in. The day was
lost. The day was dead on arrival.

You can lose many days to such exhaustion: physical exhaustion, in which you are deprived of adequate rest; emotional
exhaustion, in which you are deprived of opportunities to
release or even feel a feeling; and spiritual exhaustion, in
which you are deprived of adequate nourishment for the
soul. Exhaustion eliminates the energy needed to fully experience the gifts of the day. If you are physically exhausted,
emotionally drained, or spiritually depleted, you will be walking through life with your eyes half open, unaware of the
beauty and love around you. You will be dragging your self
through the motions, and you will be unable to move forward. You will feel like you are walking on hot tar—stuck,
going nowhere, and dead in your tracks.

Seeing the Light

Be awake. Feel rested. Feel fresh. Feel ready to start the
day. Be alert, and look for all the gifts of the day. Just
breathing in and out does not qualify as being alive. From
a spiritual perspective, being alive necessitates choosing to
be ready to receive the day.

That day at the Milwaukee Museum of Art, the bottom line
was that my group was too tired to pay attention. Paying
attention is what being spiritual is all about. All kinds of
beauty went by them that day. If you're not fully awake and

not really alert, you will not be aware of the wonderful and important things that are going on in your world.

God is found in the details of each day. There are moments of grace in every crack and crevice of the day. Paying attention is a discipline. It requires practice, but more importantly, it first requires that you are awake and aware.

Bill's Bible

"Boredom *is* lack of attention."

—Fritz Perls

Ready to Receive

Are you open? Open-hearted? Open-minded? Open to the moment? Open to others? Available? Open to the presence of God? Openness means that you are:

❖ Ready, willing, and able to feel

❖ Empathetic and compassionate

❖ Willing to change and compromise

❖ Ready to learn

❖ Enjoying the new

❖ Being nonjudgmental

❖ Not being bigoted

❖ Ready to meet the moment

❖ Ready to meet a new friend

❖ Ready to meet God

To be closed means being:

✧ Emotionally shut down

✧ Distant and detached

✧ Rigid and fixed; inflexible

✧ Resistant to learning anything new or different

✧ Critical and always skeptical

✧ Comfortable claiming some forms of bigotry

✧ Marooned in the past, or waiting for the future

✧ Unavailable today

Life is all about meeting: meeting the day, meeting a new idea, meeting with family and friends (or even a stranger), meeting the earth, and meeting God.

Spirituality is all about receiving something in those meetings. It's about letting something in, opening the door to your soul, and receiving the lessons and love. There is no point to a meeting unless something is both given and received.

You are probably quite good at the giving part. It is the receiving part that you find difficult. But spirituality is rooted in receiving—spirituality is the art of receiving.

In the Dark

If you must always be the giver, then you are unwilling to lose control. There is surrender involved in receiving. The surrender is shown in the willingness to open yourself up. To be the receiver is to wave a white flag and to claim a need to be filled.

The Gifts

Let me go out on a religious limb here. I believe that God needs you—deeply. I think that God needs you to receive. God needs you to receive the banquet He sets before you on a daily basis. I think that God needs you to be open for business, to have your soul stocked with all the wonders and lessons of being alive. I think that God weeps when He sees a "Closed" sign on the door to your heart. I think that God openly grieves when you choose to go out of the spirituality business.

Bill's Bible

"Every good gift and every perfect gift is from above."
—James 1:17

It is often difficult to receive a gift, especially an unexpected one. It feels awkward. It makes you feel uneasy. It makes you wonder what the expectation is. Are you supposed to give one in return? Is there a hidden message? Is this a come-on?

All God's gifts come unexpectedly. They are given without any expectation of return. They are given only in hope that you will receive them. To fail to receive them is to judge God harshly. The only come-on in the gifts from God is the invitation to have an affair with life.

Seeing the Light

Be open for the business of life, the business of being spiritual. Open your eyes, your heart, and your mind. Open the door to your soul. Greet the day with enthusiasm. and welcome the dawn with gratitude. To open yourself up to the wonders of the day is to open up the soul to sharing the wonders of you.

The Lessons

It was a bleak, ugly February day. It was noon, but the sky was as dark as dusk. The clouds were cold and wet and hung low. The wind was just crazy and coming from all directions. I was driving back home after dropping my son off at the Buxton School in Williamstown, Massachusetts. Driving was horrible. The visibility was next to nothing, and the wind actually rocked the car. There was nothing to look at, so it felt like I was driving down the inside of a tornado.

I turned left, heading east on Route 9, heading toward Amherst. I have a favorite restaurant there, Judie's, and I thought I deserved a break from driving through this slop. It started to sleet. I had rarely seen a more disgusting day. This was the ugly face of February, all right. As the highway climbed up one of the Berkshire mini-mountains, I became aware of the sleet turning to ice. I was driving at a crawl.

Just as I reached the crest, the sun emerged out from under two lumpy, charcoal-gray clouds. There on the top of the mountain, everything was coated in ice. The sun sent dazzling prisms off every bush, tree, house, fence, rock, or barn. The beauty was overwhelming. It was like arriving in heaven after a sojourn though hell. I stopped the car and shot five rolls of film. Everywhere I looked the beauty was breathtaking.

There it was: a lesson, an epiphany, a revelation, a message from God. Even the ugliest can be transformed into pure beauty in no more than a moment—the twinkling of an eye.

Seeing the Light

An epiphany is when God cartwheels across your path or moons you to get your attention. God will do almost anything to get noticed. God is a show-off.

Life is forever teaching. The lessons are incessant. Every moment and morsel of your life and world contains an infinite number of truths. It is your spiritual task to receive them, to be a sponge and soak them up, and to open you heart, mind, and soul to the messages being sent.

In a way, you are like one of those air traffic controllers. Messages are coming in and going out all the time. You rarely get a break. This is a job that requires practice and focus and devotion, and you have a responsibility that can save lives— or at least save yours.

Here is a brief survey for you to complete. It is meant only to get you in touch with your own level of receptivity.

In the Past Year

1. What was the most significant lesson you have learned?
2. In what ways do you feel that you have grown?
3. In what ways have you been forced to change?
4. How have you compromised?

5. How have you experienced God?

6. How have you matured spiritually?

7. How have you matured emotionally?

8. What were your most significant defeats?

9. What did you learn from those defeats?

10. Have you made any new friends?

11. Have you developed any new hobbies or interests?

12. Have you become more disciplined? How? In what ways?

13. Have you come to any conclusions or insights?

14. Have you garnered any wisdom?

15. Has your faith grown?

The Conflicts

Life begins with conflict. Like labor pains, there is the desire to stay put versus the need to come out. It isn't pretty, but it is required in all birthing experiences, whether they are physical, emotional, or spiritual. All creativity requires conflict. You resolve a conflict and move on. The movement is called maturity.

Bill's Bible

"When the fight begins within himself
a man's worth something."

—Robert Browning

If you are always running from conflict and pain, you will never learn to compromise, to change, to learn and grow—to mature. These conflicts are not sent as curses, but as opportunities. Each crisis is an opportunity to deepen, strengthen, and expand—to become firmer, simpler, finer, wiser, and more mature. Maturation is a refiner's fire. You prove your metal by embracing the conflicting issues of your life.

Spirituality is a creative process. It is the process of creating meaning in life. It is the art of revealing the divine within the human. Creativity requires a safe context where conflict can take place. For you, that is the soul. The soul is the place where you must sort out your values, morals, beliefs, and dreams.

If you have lost touch with your soul, you will be unable to create. You cannot create friendship or faith, love or hope, community or the Kingdom. You will never grapple with what concerns you ultimately. You will never resolve who you are, how you feel called, or what you hope your legacy will be. A lifeless soul cannot keep bringing you back to life. A lifeless soul can only destroy.

In the Dark

You cannot avoid conflict forever. The time wasted avoiding or trying to ignore conflict is longer than eternity. You must embrace conflict. Receive crisis as an opportunity. You will be fertilizing your soul and readying that soul for major growth and maturation.

In the Bible, you are told to pick up your crosses and follow. Now, that is not a real pleasant thought or plan. Nobody is real keen on being crucified. Still, the biblical message is clear:

You can't avoid the difficult times of life. You can't avoid pain. There is no way to be fully alive without also being willing to dive fully into the midst of life's many conflicts and crises. Like it or not, pain always reminds you of your humanness, and it is your humanness that intimately connects you with God.

If you are to be fully alive, you must be willing to know pain. You must be willing to enter the bull ring of conflict. You must be ready to stare down a crisis. To be fully alive is to be fully mature, and maturation cannot occur without a significant parade of conflicts to resolve.

Living to Love

Love is beautiful. Love is difficult. Love is an art that requires daily practice. Love is the energy that supplies life with purpose. Love is spirituality's top prize. Love is a huge risk. The risk is that what you love, you may lose. Love does end. At times, it ends mercifully, and at other times, quite brutally. The loss of love can be devastating. It is a pain that goes deep and is a hurt that penetrates to the soul.

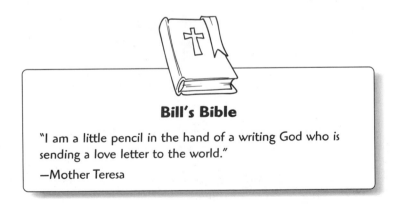

Bill's Bible

"I am a little pencil in the hand of a writing God who is sending a love letter to the world."
—Mother Teresa

Falling in love is worse yet. The risk here is in the falling. Romantic love involves an almost complete loss of control. You will feel need as you never have before. You will know a passionate drive to be understood. You will experience a desire to be one with someone, to lose yourself within the safety of another's love. You will want to spend endless hours together. You will feel as though you can never get enough time, talk, or touch, and that you will never get enough of being told that you are loved. It is an overwhelming, even frightening, experience.

Still, it is love that gives life to life itself. It is love that makes the conflicts, crises, problems, and pain worth the effort. It is love that most refreshes and restores the soul. If you want to be fully alive, there is no turning away from the demand to love and be loved.

When you love and are loved, you will feel closest to God. You will sense God's presence in all acts of genuine love. You will feel as if you are sharing heart and mind and soul with God.

It is God's wish that you learn to fall in love thousands of times. God wants you to fall in love with the stars and the sea, the flowers and the seasons, birds and animals, and people of all races, colors, and creeds. God wants you to love the all of life—every morsel, every drop.

Bill's Bible

"The love we give away is the only love we keep."
—Elbert Hubbard

Indeed, what the world needs is love—lots and lots of it. In the eyes of God, love cannot fail, for to love is to be exactly who you were created to be. Love is the answer. Love is the price we pay to be alive. Love is the wages we receive, and it is more than a fair deal.

The Least You Need to Know

✧ To be alive is a choice. You can also choose to deaden your self.

✧ To be alive means to be awake, alert, and aware. It is to be open for the business of living, loving, and learning— spirituality.

✧ To be alive is to be ready for meeting the gifts and the pains of the day.

✧ To be fully alive is to be fully committed to the art of loving.

✧ The art of loving requires daily practice and discipline.

Chapter 11

Be Hopeful

In This Chapter

❖ What hope *is*

❖ What can make us hope-full

❖ How to build the hope habit

❖ How to keep it positive and keep your hopes high

❖ How little things can make a big difference: common sense, patience, hard work, imagination, humor, and faith

Just this past Christmas season, I asked my youth what their hopes were for their futures. They spoke of things like owning a Porsche, sailing the Mediterranean on their own schooner, or winning the lottery. I explained to them that these were not hopes. These were goals, dreams, and even expectations. But that they did not qualify as hopes.

They looked confused. "Why not?" was the question on their faces and minds. I tried to break down the concept of hope for them in the following manner:

❖ Hope is not stuff.

❖ Hope is not an expectation or a demand.

✧ Hope is not found out there.

✧ Hope is something that comes from within.

✧ Hope is a product of your soul.

✧ Hope is a spiritual choice.

✧ Hope is a perspective, a way of seeing the world.

✧ Hope is an attitude, a way of choosing to experience the world.

✧ Hope must be intimately connected to that world.

✧ Hope must make you and your world better.

✧ Hope makes a world of difference.

Hope is not easy. Hope is not cheap. Hope is seldom something sweet. Hope is a passion, a willingness to sweat and suffer, a burning desire. Hope is an inner belief in the goodness of the world and in everyone and everything in it. Hope is a faith in creation and the Creator. Hope is believing that God knew what God was doing when you were created human, when God created you. Hope is a confidence in the ultimate wisdom of God.

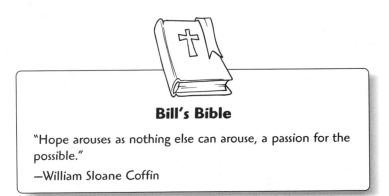

Bill's Bible

"Hope arouses as nothing else can arouse, a passion for the possible."

—William Sloane Coffin

What Makes Us Hope-Full?

Hope is found within you—in the real you who has chosen to be fully alive and who is open and ready to meet the day.

Hope is found within the you whose soul is properly prepared to pay attention to the lessons, crises, and gifts of each
day. And hope is found within the you who is equipped to
squeeze out all the living, loving, and learning that you can.

Hope can be *inspired* by witnessing an act of courage, kindness, or mercy. When you are deeply moved by the raw love
you experience in someone's actions, the goodness and decency, the soul moved to a new, more hope-filled attitude.
Inspiration is to be moved spiritually. A shift in the soul does
not need an earthquake; it merely needs to be reminded of
the beauty and blessing that can be found in every day, right
here and right now.

Bill's Bible

"When you get to the end of your rope, tie a knot and
hang on."

—Anonymous

Hope can be *ignited*. The fuel for hope is often tears. What
moves you to tears? Beauty? Awe? Reverence? Compassion?
Love? Tears speak a deep truth. Tears tell of a soul that is im-
mersed in the goodness of the moment. Tears speak of the joy
to be found in every meeting. It's ironic, but tears ignite the
soul to care passionately about the gifts of the day. Tears burn
bright with hope.

Hope can be *infused*. If you are spiritually empty, the flame of
the spirit will have gone out. Those are the times that you
feel as if life is nothing but more and more work, with less
and less pleasure. There is nothing to look forward to and
nothing to get excited about. Those are hopeless times. At

such times, you will need an infusion of spirit, and this infusion must come from God. Only God can restore your hopeful attitude and perspective. You must be ready to receive the transfusion from God's spirit to your spirit.

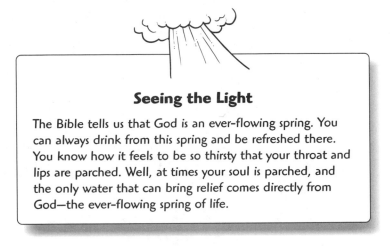

Seeing the Light

The Bible tells us that God is an ever-flowing spring. You can always drink from this spring and be refreshed there. You know how it feels to be so thirsty that your throat and lips are parched. Well, at times your soul is parched, and the only water that can bring relief comes directly from God—the ever-flowing spring of life.

I am not speaking of a specific miracle here, because all of life is a miracle. There is a miracle in every moment. The issue here is whether you are ready to consciously let God in, to let God help, and to let go and let God. The hope is always God's to give, but sometimes you must be willing to ask to receive the gift.

The infusion of hope comes most often from prayer and worship. It comes when you devote time and space to receiving, listening, and learning. It comes when you choose to be on your knees, confessing your need, asking for help, and patiently waiting to receive. When you are in the spiritual posture of receptivity, God will arrive. That is the promise of all prayer and worship.

Hope is not about hearing the answer that you want or expect God to give. Hope is in receiving whatever God chooses to give. Hope is in trusting God to be present in the day. Hope is turning over the controls to God.

Building the Hope Habit

Hope is the heart's choice of attitude and perspective. It is the soul's choice of priorities and daily decisions. The heart and soul can't get enough of it.

One of the first ways to build the hope habit is to become aware of your own level of hope—who and what inspires it, and where do you most often find it. You must become aware of the reality of hope in your life. Don't assume it. Don't ignore it. Try to keep it in focus and pay attention to how it works. What gives it a pulse? What gets the hope passion flowing in your veins?

Here is a good beginning to building the hope habit. Answer these questions honestly and openly. Take your time:

✧ How do you hope to change in the next year?

✧ How do you hope that your parents and family will change?

✧ What are your hopes for your education?

✧ What are your hopes for your faith?

✧ What hopes do you have for your friends? Have you shared these with them?

✧ What hopes do you have for the world you live in?

✧ How do you try to live out those hopes?

✧ Have you ever felt hopeless? When? Why?

✧ How did you handle it?

✧ Who inspires hope in you?

✧ What inspires hope in you?

✧ Do you know anyone who is feeling hopeless?

✧ How might you help this person?

In the Dark

Being hopeless is choosing to be closed to others, the world, your own soul, and maybe—especially—God.

Keep It Positive

Every congregation has a few souls in it that I am convinced even Jesus wouldn't like. I really mean that. These folks are always whining and moaning about something. They never mean to complain; they just call it being honest. Real honesty, though, is never exclusively negative. Their brand of honesty never includes a compliment or affirmation.

When these folks walk into a committee meeting, an adult education class, or even worship, they make me tired. Just to be in their presence is exhausting. Their negative energy can sap the spirit right out of me. I hate to admit it, but I try to avoid them. I just don't want to be near this negativity.

Whenever I do have to spend a couple hours with one of these individuals, I can feel the hope literally draining out of my being. Their negativity and scapegoating and finger-pointing leave my soul slumped in a corner. There is just no way to fight back. The only way to retrieve the hope is to leave and refuel.

Negativity kills hope in these ways:

✧ By greeting the day with a grimace

✧ By seeing the day as empty of purpose and promise

✧ By looking only for the flaw and failing in others

✧ By keeping track of mistakes

✧ By always feeling like a victim

✧ By expecting God to give only the answers you want to hear

If you are serious about building up the hope habit in yourself, then you will need to keep it positive. Keeping it positive means ...

✧ Greeting the day with a smile, and as a welcome guest.

✧ Looking for the good in life.

✧ Trying to point out the good in others.

✧ Trying to bring out the best in others.

✧ Giving your best.

✧ Refusing to pawn your problems off on others or use anyone as a scapegoat.

✧ Refusing to be a bigot.

✧ Searching for the God in others.

✧ Searching for the God in your world and in your self.

✧ Always being excited about the day's potential.

✧ Always being open to the new.

✧ Showing reverence and respect for the old, wherever it is due.

✧ Treating time as a precious gift.

✧ Treating each moment as a potential miracle.

✧ Trying to create heaven here on Earth.

Bill's Bible

"You cannot do a kindness too soon, for you never know how soon it will be too late."

—Ralph Waldo Emerson

Keeping it positive creates hope. It builds hope. It gives hope a chance. Keeping it positive is not about acting as if you are certain to have it your way; it is knowing that you trust however it will turn out. A positive attitude is being willing to wait because you believe that something good and beautiful is just around the corner.

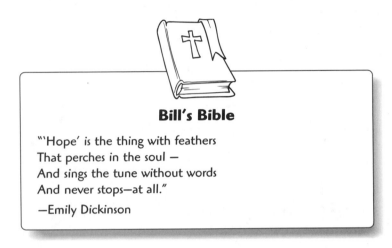

Bill's Bible

"'Hope' is the thing with feathers
That perches in the soul —
And sings the tune without words
And never stops—at all."

—Emily Dickinson

You Can Be Kind

One of the basics of the hope habit is simple human kindness. At times, your world must seem overwhelmingly complex. You must often ask yourself how you can make any real difference, or how you can help sort out the world's many messes. I think that your whole generation shouts at the world "What can I really do about it?"

Here's one answer: You can be kind. This is not an easy answer. It is simply an answer that works and breeds hope. It is an answer that enables hope to happen.

Shelter Island has only a few stores—even fewer in the winter, when many of them close up for the season. Every December, the youth group and I go on a Christmas shopping trip to a mall nearly two hours away. The youth count on this trip and look forward to it. They usually do fairly well at saving their money. Unfortunately, most of them do most of their shopping for themselves instead of getting Christmas gifts for others. I know you can relate.

Within the first hour of shopping, Michael lost his wallet, or had it stolen. He left it, he thought, on top of a game in the video arcade. He had brought along $130 to spend. Everyone felt bad for him, but not one youth volunteered a dime. I was disappointed. I knew they expected me to bail him out—in truth, I would have, but I wanted to see if they would respond.

Each hour we met to check in. At the next check-in time, Peter gave Michael half his money: $50. This act of kindness was significant because Peter and Michael had never been friends. In fact, they sort of disliked each other. It was also significant because Michael's three best friends initially had not offered Michael a cent, but now they were inspired to fork over a few bucks as well. By the time Michael collected all the donations, he had $140. Everyone, including Peter, told him he did not have to pay them back.

Kindness is contagious. Kindness inspires goodness. Goodness inspires hope. You can be kind—it is often more than enough.

Ordered Priorities

The hope habit has well-ordered priorities. Hope clearly knows what matters, what is of lasting value, and what is eternal in worth. At times I am astonished by what people choose as their top priorities. Many folks seem to care most about their appearance, about what they own, about who they know, or about where they have been. It's a shame to make a priority out of that which cannot last and, ultimately, that does nothing of any real good for anyone—not even you.

Ask yourself the following questions about priorities. You will find this brief questionnaire to be difficult but insightful.

Ordering My Priorities

1. What was your top priority for today?
2. What was your top priority last year?
3. Did you accomplish it?
4. What are your father's top priorities in life? What are your mother's?
5. Who do you feel has priorities in order? Why?
6. What are your top priorities for the near future?
7. How would God rearrange your priorities?
8. How would you rearrange the priorities of your two best friends?
9. What are the top priorities of most Americans?
10. How would God hope to rearrange those?

Priorities are statements. They state your values. They state your principles. They make decisions. They define your day and how it will be spent. Priorities clearly declare your hopes.

In the Dark

To make money, looks, or things your top priority is to rob the soul of any chance to declare a genuine hope. The soul simply cannot be heard over all the noise you are making trying to scramble up that ladder of success.

Making a Difference

You live in a culture that is addicted to all things big. Bigger is better. Our nation is childish in its pursuit of the biggest gifts with the flashiest packaging. As a nation, we tend to overlook the lovely gifts that come in small, unwrapped boxes. God does not overlook these gifts, though. God is forever trying to gain our attention and to point out the value of the little things in life.

God is always informing you of what will ultimately be remembered: your kindness and generosity; your compassion and passion; your depth, sensitivity, and wisdom; your attitude and perspective; your priorities and beliefs; your willingness to serve and sacrifice; and your gentle spirit and gracious soul. These are not little things. In God's eyes, they are huge. They are what can grant you a big boost of hope.

Think about your own parents. They may be just ordinary folks in the eyes of the world. Maybe they have not accomplished anything that has made them famous or allowed them to achieve celebrity status. Maybe they will never see their names recorded in a history book. However, in your eyes, they have accomplished some extraordinarily important things: creating a home, being there for you night and day, and taking seriously their responsibility to raise you right. They may never get credit from the world for all the sacrifices they have made on your behalf, but in your eyes, it has made all the difference. (Tell them!)

In God's eyes, the ordinary is best equipped to be extraordinary. The things you think of as common are often packed with uncommon wisdom. Being average is to have passed with honors.

A Little Common Sense

A little common sense can make a big difference. Common sense is stepping back and looking at the whole picture. Common sense is trusting what you already know. Common sense is knowing that history does repeat itself and that humans are prone to making the same mistakes over and over again. Common sense is God-given wisdom. Common sense is when you trust your heart to inform you of the truth, your soul to guide you in the right direction, and your God to get you there safe and sound. A little common sense can turn chaos into creativity—hope!

Tim came to me a week before Valentine's Day. For the past few months, he'd had a big-time crush on Sara. Sara was mildly interested in him, but she was shy and not sure that she really wanted to get into a serious relationship. Tim had bought her a beautiful, expensive necklace and a card the size of Utah, and he was planning to send a dozen long-stemmed pink roses—pink was Sara's favorite color.

"What do you think?" Tim asked me.

"She's not the Christ child," I said.

"You mean it's too much?" Tim again asked.

"Tim, think about it for a second."

Tim did think about it. He paused for no more than a minute or two, and then said "I guess it would be overwhelming to get so much. I mean, we really aren't even dating yet."

Bingo! Common sense. The hope of dating Sara had been restored. He sent a single rose, with a brief note. They are still dating.

A Little Patience

A little patience can make a big difference. Patience does not throw up its hands and give up, but it keeps the hands busy untying the knots of life. You will do your best work when you are relaxed. A relaxed soul is ready to run the race at a steady pace. A relaxed soul can focus and grant dexterity to the fingers. A relaxed soul creates a patient spirit. A patient spirit makes peace.

A rushed soul is distracted and easily annoyed. A harried soul is clumsy and careless. A hassled soul is one that is at war with itself and one that creates only chaos—a mess.

Just think of how many problems you could have avoided by simply taking your time. Think of the relationships that could have been salvaged by having patiently thought things through, before having spoken or acted. Think of how many opportunities have been wasted by trying to do too much too soon, by not giving yourself the time to gain the skill, the knowledge, or the wisdom necessary to accomplish the task. You need patience because hope takes time and is created by perseverance. Hope has no use for a clock because it is never alarmed.

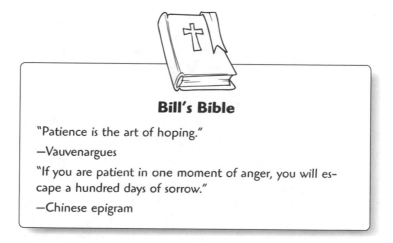

Bill's Bible

"Patience is the art of hoping."

—Vauvenargues

"If you are patient in one moment of anger, you will escape a hundred days of sorrow."

—Chinese epigram

A Little Hard Work

A little hard work can make a big difference. Let's say that you have a paper to write. You sit around trying to figure out what to write. You call a few friends to complain about how stupid the assignment is. You listen to a few tunes to forget about it for a while. You go to the refrigerator and make a huge snack. You notice that the TV's on, and you eat your snack while watching a show. You start to think of excuses to tell the teacher. You begin to plan how to fool your parents into letting you stay home—you are soooo sick.

You are struck by a sudden bolt of self-respect, and you head up to your room. You go to your desk, get out the paper and pen and the books you will need. You tell yourself to just start writing. The first few sentences are tough. You can feel yourself getting frustrated, but you stick with it. Suddenly, the writing is coming easier. You are into it. Like figuring out the combination to a lock, you have now somehow gotten inside, and the writing really takes off.

In a few hours of nonstop work, the paper is done. You feel tired, but you're pleased. You reread it. It's good—damn good. You are excited about turning it in. You feel confident of getting a good mark. You are proud of yourself. Strangely, even your future feels more secure. Guess what just happened? Hope!

What a difference a little hard work can make. As the infamous ad says "Just do it!" Hope is an action.

A Little Imagination

With 40 people, the ecumenical youth group was larger than usual this particular Sunday evening. I asked them all to take off their shoes, find an open space on the Fellowship Hall carpet, and lie on their backs. They did so—laughing, of course. I explained to them that I wanted to do a guided meditation and that I needed them to trust both me and their imaginations to do all the work. I explained that the meditation would require them to be absolutely quiet and still, and that any noise or distraction could ruin the whole experience. I rarely plead for their cooperation, but I am sure that the tone of my voice told them that I was being serious and sincere in my request.

The room grew quickly quiet, with just a cough or a giggle or two. I asked them to shut their eyes and to take 10 deep breaths. I explained that I needed them to relax and focus. The guided meditation began. A guided mediation goes into great detail so that the experience is as vivid as possible. Without taking you through the whole meditation, let me tell you the gist of it: They went to New York City for a physical exam with a doctor they did not know, but who had been recommended by a doctor here on the island. The physical exam reveals some terrible news: They have an inoperable cancerous tumor. Their life expectancy is no more than a year.

After leaving the doctor's office, they are invited to imagine how everything looked and felt. They are asked to imagine what they thought about on the long bus ride home. They are asked to imagine how their homes and rooms would look when they returned; who the first person would be that they told; how they would break it to their families; what they would do that night; and what they would pray for in the days ahead.

The meditation concluded with them being told that they are fine and healthy and here on Shelter Island. Slowly they are asked to return to reality. The group arose, animated and dazed—clearly anxious to talk about the experience. For nearly three hours, we unpacked the experience:

✧ They were stunned by how real it all felt.

✧ Most of them initially refused to believe the doctor.

✧ They left the doctor's office feeling angry, anxious, and bewildered.

✧ They were amazed at the brightness of everything outside.

✧ They spoke eloquently of the Earth's simple beauties: the sky, the clouds, the trees, the colors, the wind, and the sun.

✧ They spoke with love about their homes and rooms.

✧ They spoke with love about their families and friends.

✧ They spoke with deep, deep appreciation for the parents (or parent) who, they knew would help them through this.

✧ They immediately knew their best friends, and many were shocked to realize that they had let these friendships fall apart.

✧ They were conscious of a deepening faith and feeling close to God.

✧ They were so aware of the preciousness of life.

✧ They were determined to fight and win their health.

✧ They *all* refused to give up hope.

All this came from a little imagination. This guided meditation appeared to be about death, but it wound up unlocking a passion for living and is an experience of how the imagination can create hope.

A Little Humor

Worship can get dull—too serious, too heavy, and too religiousy. I long ago came to the conclusion that worship needs to have a good sense of humor. A laughing congregation is a loving congregation. A church family that gets the joke will become a true community that can honestly and humanly care about each other.

I always try to share something funny in worship. I see it as a dose of humanity; a dose of humility, because most jokes are on or about our human foibles; and a dose of healing, because laughter does wonders in curing the soul of its ills and creating a good deal of hope.

A Little Faith

The loss of Christopher Tehan to brain cancer at age 13 has been the most devastating experience in my ministry to the youth here. Never have I witnessed someone so young fight a disease with so much maturity and dignity. Never have I watched a family show such great love and support. Even on the day that the cancer had robbed Christopher of his sight, his response was to ask about computers for blind kids, and to ask whether they made 10-speed tandem bikes so that his friends could ride up front while he pedaled in the rear. I wish he were still around. We all prayed for a miracle. Little did we know the miracle was already in front of us: Christopher's hope and faith.

Bill's Bible

"Faith is knowing there is an ocean because you have seen a brook."

—William Arthur Ward

When Christopher's friends gathered for the wake, many were terrified to go inside the funeral parlor. They did not want to see Christopher in a casket. They did not want to see death up close and personal. They did not want to confront the fragility and uncertainty of life. I totally understood.

I asked them to join hands with me and pray. Not knowing what else to do, they did as I asked. It was a short prayer. I asked for God to be there with us and to surround us with His/Her love and compassion. I asked God to take good care of Christopher and to enjoy him as much as we all had. I thanked God for the gift of Christopher's life. I thanked God for a miracle named Christopher. Since Christopher was an avid and terrific golfer, I also told God that He/She would have to take up the game.

The prayer helped them. The prayer helped me. We all went inside. We cried. We stared and sobbed. We prayed again. We hugged his mom and dad and sister, Andrea. That little prayer had given us the faith necessary to go inside and the faith required to believe that Christopher was now on the other side—hope!

The Least You Need to Know

✧ Hope is a choice, an attitude, and a perspective.

✧ Hope needs to become a habit in your life.

✧ The hope habit lifts the spirit and makes you want to seek out ways to improve the world.

✧ It takes only a little common sense, patience, hard work, imagination, humor, and faith to make a big difference in the quality of your life.

Part 4

Living the Genuine Good Life

When did being good become bad in our culture? When was it that the so-called good life was no longer connected to good-ness? How was it that the idea of being a genuinely good human being became equated to being a "goody two shoes" or a "holy roller"?

A spiritual life is in pursuit of the genuine good life. It seeks goodness—real goodness. It believes that without goodness, Life is empty; Life is void of meaning; Life is without hope. A genuine good life is one that is intimately connected to chasing those things that are literally good for you. The goal of a gen-uine good life is to become a good-for-everything.

Have you heard your parents use the phrase "goodness knows"? That is a phrase with a lot of history. It means exactly what it says. Goodness knows what matters. Goodness knows what is right. Goodness knows the Truth. Goodness knows the will of God. Goodness knows how to love and forgive. Goodness knows. *That is a phrase that belongs in your everyday lan-guage. It is a maxim you need to memorize.*

Chapter 12

Who Am I?

In This Chapter

✧ The ways in which you will need to thoroughly explore your inner universe, and the obstacles you may find doing so

✧ How to explore your roots

✧ Why you are not something to be found, but created; why you are not meant to be normal, but natural

✧ Why the only real success is to live your life in your own way

✧ How you are not called to success, but to being faithful to your own truth

Adolescence is a stage of life dominated by an identity crisis. Two words are key here: First is *identity:* who you are, what makes you *you,* what you stand for, and who you are determined to become. Second is *crisis:* The need to know yourself is urgent; it is a struggle; and it will take all of who you are to resolve.

An identity crisis is like a bad oil spill—it seems to always be expanding. It may appear at first to be no big deal, but once it washes up on the shore of your life, it can just about ruin everything. The damage done can last forever.

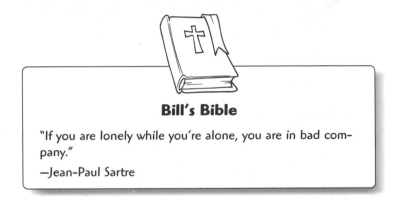

Bill's Bible

"If you are lonely while you're alone, you are in bad company."
—Jean-Paul Sartre

As an adolescent, you are like a trapeze artist. You are leaving one safe perch (childhood) to travel to another safe perch (adulthood). The flight on the trapeze is the identity crisis, and at present you may be working without a net.

Spirituality can be your net. Spirituality can provide you the safety and security you need to risk the leap. The leap of faith should never be taken without a net—that's just plain foolish. That is for dare-devils, and most dare-devils never make it to the other side—of anything.

An identity crisis will force you to ask many difficult but vital questions. These are not questions you are being asked to answer, but to live. You must immerse yourself in the question. You must learn to swim in its depths. These questions will open up a whole new world to you: the universe that exists within you.

The key question raised by an identity crisis is, "Who am I?" It is a question that paradoxically may seem as enormous as a galaxy and as puny as an ant. It is a question that serves as a catalyst for a hunt.

"Who am I?" is a question that will set you off on a remarkable journey of discovery. It is a quest to uncover what you really feel, think, and believe. It is a search for your very own soul. Although the question can never be answered fully, if you are to enter adulthood, you must feel reasonably confident that you are doing a good job in living your answer.

Bill's Bible

"If you don't stand for something, you'll fall for anything."
—Michael Evans

Exploring the Inner Universe

Where do you look to find your self? You must look inside. You must rummage around in your mind's attic and discover your own thoughts. You must explore the secret chamber of your heart and discover the depths of your emotions. You must dig for the buried treasure of your beliefs. You must examine and explore your whole inner universe.

You will face many obstacles to this exploration, chief among them being your own anxiety about looking inside. Anxiety is like fear, but without an object. If you are out walking and hear a big dog barking, you will probably cross the street (which is dumb—like dogs can't cross streets!) due to your fear. The object of your fear is the dog. With anxiety, there is the same level of fear, but no object. You don't know what you are afraid of; you just know that you feel uptight and tense all over.

Why would you be nervous about looking inside? I mean, really, what's the big deal? I think you are anxious simply because it is uncharted territory. Most of you have spent so little time alone with yourself that your own inner world is seen as some dense dangerous jungle, full of wild animals and slithering, fork-tongued creatures.

Have you ever traveled to a country that speaks a language you don't understand or speak? To be a foreigner is an anxious experience. You don't feel grounded. You feel totally uprooted. You feel like you have just been thrown out of a plane without a parachute. The anxiety can feel like a free-fall.

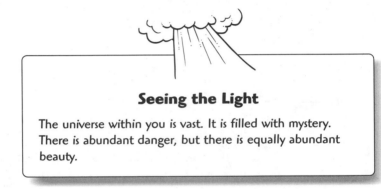

Seeing the Light

The universe within you is vast. It is filled with mystery. There is abundant danger, but there is equally abundant beauty.

For many of you, if not most of you, your inner world will make you feel like that foreigner. You will be struggling to find your way. You will get frustrated by the difficulty in communicating the simplest needs. You will be swept by a homesickness that will leave you spiritually paralyzed. You will just want to get out of there and go back home.

In this case, home is your image. You feel at home being defined by what you wear, the car you drive, what your grades are, what sports you play, what your parents do for a living, where you live, where you plan to attend college, and how much success and beauty and stuff you can claim to own. Home is where you are defined exclusively by external appearances. You feel safe and at ease there. You belong. You are being a typical teenager, defined by your world, your parents, and your peers.

To be forced to go inside and to define your own self is a frightening challenge. You are terrified of being alone, which is the only way to make the journey. You are worried that you are going to be terribly homesick. You hate feeling like a foreigner. You can't see any purpose for the trip because it does not sound like a vacation. Daily you try to find an excuse to get out of going.

In the Dark

If you choose to leave your inner universe unvisited and unexplored, you will have chosen to let your soul shrink and shrivel. You will lose contact with God, with your deepest needs and wishes, with your hopes and dreams, and with everything that could make your life worth the living.

To be honest, the journey inside is risky—it is a leap of faith. There are some hidden and even obvious dangers. You will encounter your feelings there, and some of these can be pretty wild—like rage and envy. You will have to deal with some scary thoughts—like asking yourself if it is all worth it. There are also some sins to contend with, and a few secrets will probably leap out and scare you half to death.

Yes, there are some good reasons to feel anxious.

And yet, there are even better reasons to go, to make the trip, to experience the adventure:

✧ You will gain insight into why you feel the way you feel.

✧ You will learn about why you do what you do.

✧ You will discover your gifts and talents.

✧ You will discover your wishes and dreams.

✧ You will gain confidence in yourself.

✧ You will gain insight into others.

✧ You will become more sensitive.

✧ You will become stronger and more able to handle life's tough times.

✧ You will find courage you did not know you possessed.

✧ You will find an inner core that is called to do important things.

✧ You will become wiser and more able to overcome compulsive or out-of-control behavior.

✧ You will feel closer to those you love.

✧ You will feel closer to God.

✧ You will learn to love yourself.

✧ You will learn how to enjoy your own company.

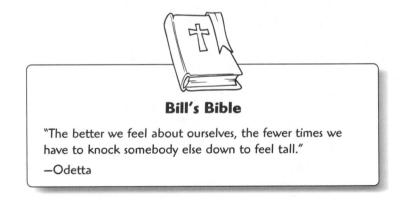

Bill's Bible

"The better we feel about ourselves, the fewer times we have to knock somebody else down to feel tall."

—Odetta

Roots

Imagine that you are attending a family reunion. A photographer has been hired to take a formal family portrait. Your grandparents and parents, uncles and aunts, cousins and siblings, and nieces and nephews are all there. Think of this gathering of familiar faces. All the history, all that genetic stuff, has been drawn together in that one place.

This family portrait is indelibly imprinted upon your soul. You carry with you the historical markers left by several generations of family. You may not believe that, or wish to believe that, but it is true. This does not mean that you are a predetermined being, but it does mean that you will be prone to certain attitudes, behaviors, and even beliefs. It is in your makeup. It is in the genes. It is in the parenting style adopted for years by your family. Many of your tendencies were authored by your upbringing. You *are* a family portrait. The family resemblance you bear on the outside is not nearly as startling as the one you carry on the inside.

In the Dark

To fail to know and understand your roots is to fail to know and understand the species of plant you are destined to become. You will not know how to properly tend to the garden of your soul.

Triumphs

At holiday time, most families gather around a table to swap family stories. These stories are rich with the distinct flavor of your clan. They are coated in your family's faith, hope, and love. All such stories are extravagantly embellished, but the family knows that the embellishments are even more real than the story itself. Usually, these stories tell of your family's triumphs: times of great courage and heroism, acts of kindness and generosity, and deeds of grace and mercy. Often, these stories reveal a family's ability to laugh at itself, which is a triumph all its own, a victory over the forces of reality.

What are the family triumphs that have become legend in your family?

Tragedies

All families experience tragedy—some more than others, and some with seemingly brutal injustice. The tragedies become either family stories or secrets. As secrets, these tragedies threaten to deeply wound and scar your soul. They endanger your spirit by gagging your inner voice and refusing to hear your screams. As stories, the tragedies regain the capacity to create courage within you, to carve in you a deep inner strength, a firm resolve that you can face and handle just about anything.

Some of the most common family tragedies are these:

✧ Physical abuse.

✧ Alcoholism and drug abuse.

✧ Sexual abuse and indiscretions. Incest is an enormous issue in our culture.

✧ Spiritual abuse, in which a person is not allowed to find and live his or her own faith.

✧ Divorce.

✧ Mental illness or emotional problems.

✧ Death—especially by accident or at the hands of violence, or of a baby or child.

✧ Financial failure.

✧ Educational failure.

✧ Illegal activity.

✧ Compulsive behaviors—gambling, overeating, anorexia, bulimia, and so on.

✧ Betrayals.

✧ Shattered dreams.

What are the tragedies of your family history? How have they impacted your family and the way its members function? Are they kept as secrets or revealed as sacred stories?

Truths

In my family, certain truths were the unspoken code of our family. I never recognized this code until I got into therapy in college. The following was the Grimbol Code of Conduct:

- ✧ A Grimbol should never be angry.
- ✧ A Grimbol should never be wrong.
- ✧ A Grimbol should always put others first.
- ✧ A Grimbol should be generous to a fault.
- ✧ A Grimbol should not need help with emotional issues.
- ✧ A Grimbol must never think too highly of himself.
- ✧ A Grimbol should identify with the little guy.
- ✧ A Grimbol should always be happy with what he gets.
- ✧ A Grimbol is never lucky.
- ✧ A Grimbol longs for the good old days, when the people and life were better.

Over the years, these truths have been both a blessing and a curse in my life. This is the case for all family codes of conduct. Sometimes they work wonders. Sometimes they wreak havoc. It has taken me a long time to adjust and alter that code of conduct so that it offers me a better chance at health and happiness.

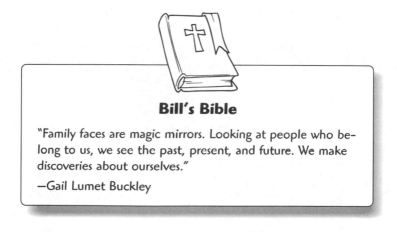

Bill's Bible

"Family faces are magic mirrors. Looking at people who belong to us, we see the past, present, and future. We make discoveries about ourselves."

—Gail Lumet Buckley

What is the silent code of conduct of your family? What are the truths to which your family unconsciously clings?

Your roots run deep. You are grounded in family history. Your soul is planted in the soil of your family's perspective on life. You need to intimately know where you came from. You need to know your family members' concerns and convictions; their causes and passions; their flaws and failings; their hopes and dreams; and their secret disappointments and griefs. You need to know them in order to know you. You need to know them in order to decide the *you* that you wish to become. Not all family resemblance is genetic—much of it is choice.

Am I Normal?

Sadly, what fuels the identity crisis is the rampant belief that you must be normal. Your idea of normal is defined by your parents' expectations, the fashions and values of your peers, and the whims of the mass media. The original question, "Who am I?" which possesses unlimited potential for spiritual growth, is transformed into the inquiry "Am I normal?" which has no potential at all for spiritual growth—in fact, quite the opposite, for most teenagers answer this question by living lives that diminish their spirituality.

The more you try to be normal, the less you are yourself. The more you try to pour yourself into what you perceive as the normal mold, you wind up confining and restricting your spirit. In most adolescents that I know, an increase in normalcy is accompanied with a dramatic decrease in spiritual integrity.

In the Dark

If you have made normalcy your God, you will be worshipping in a sanctuary called rut and at an altar called boredom.

Normal Isn't Normal

I am always amazed at how upset adults get by adolescent rebellion. Although it is supposedly normal for an adolescent to rebel, you are never expected to do so. Parents get furious when you challenge a rule or belief. Teachers are offended if you disagree. Priests, ministers, and rabbis are confounded by your seeming lack of faith—their faith. Though it is natural for a teenager to rebel, you live in a culture that has declared it unacceptable.

That is the whole problem with normal—nobody knows what it is. It never seems to stay the same. What is normal for one person is the opposite for another. What can be safely said about normal is that normal tries to be safe, secure, and convenient, and never rock the boat. Normal should keep everyone happy.

If you are going to be a spiritual person, you cannot be so-called normal. Spirituality does not play it safe. It does not try to keep everyone happy. And it is always rocking the boat.

Normal Isn't Extraordinary

I am regularly reminded that many of you have extraordinary expectations of your self, your world, and your life. You are quite certain that your life will be filled with extraordinary adventures, accomplishments, pleasures, and possessions. Normal for you is the good life, and you fully expect to get your big piece of the pie. You might see it as your right or as your inheritance. Anything less than the best is just not good enough. You fully expect life to be lived on your terms, and those are all about your guarantee to the good life.

May I remind you that normal is not extraordinary. Life does not offer you or anyone else any guarantee of fame or fortune. If you inherit your fame and fortune, just consider yourself the lucky recipient of aristocratic welfare—which is not normal.

The spiritual life is all about being ordinary, about the basic goodness and beauty to be found in the most ordinary things, and about the fact that God unveils the most extraordinary truths in the most ordinary lives. Ordinary is special. Ordinary is enough. Ordinary is what reveals the excellence of God's creation. Creation is extraordinary. The Creator is extraordinary.

Normal Isn't Perfect

You will make mistakes—big ones. You will flop—big time. You will be defeated—often. You will be disappointed—repeatedly. You will be hurt—more than you deserve. You will face numerous losses—they will threaten to make you bitter. You will know sadness and sorrow—intimately. You will tell lies; you will be lied to. You will be mocked; you will mock. You will betray God. You will sin and suffer, and be forced to serve and sacrifice, even when you do not want to. This is life. This *is* normal. This is no big deal. Trying to be perfect is foolish. The pursuit of perfection always leads to disappointment, so instead try excellence. Pursue being your best—*that* will be inspiring.

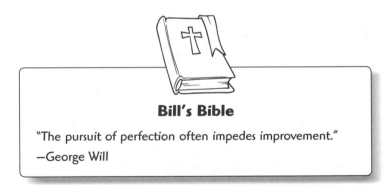

Bill's Bible

"The pursuit of perfection often impedes improvement."

—George Will

Be Natural

The best answer you can give to the question "Who am I?" is to be who you are. Be yourself. Be real, genuine, and natural. To be natural is to be true to the yearnings of your soul. To be natural is to follow your bliss. To be natural is to trust that you not only know who you are, but that you also know where you are going. It is believing in yourself and living that way. It is respecting your will and wishes, and letting them take the lead.

To be natural is as instinctual as the migration of birds. Birds know when the climate is getting bad and when it is time to move on. They know exactly when to leave, where they are going, and how to get there. So do you. Listen to your heart.

Will I Be a Success?

You live in a culture that advocates answering the question "Who am I?" with what you do for a living or how much you earn. You are constantly hammered with ideals, like "You are what you do," "You are worth what you make," and "You must be a success to be a somebody."

As you know by now, I am a minister. I have performed hundreds of funerals. Trust me, nobody is remembered for what they do for a living or how much they earn or own. People are remembered only for their integrity and dignity, the depth and loyalty of their friendships, and the courage and grace with which they lived. Success in life is measured in love.

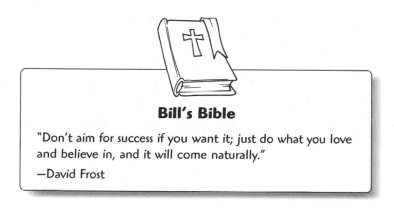

Bill's Bible

"Don't aim for success if you want it; just do what you love and believe in, and it will come naturally."

—David Frost

The Least You Need to Know

❖ Who you are is found within, in the inner universe that contains your heart and soul.

❖ You hesitate to go inside because it makes you feel uneasy. You must overcome that uneasiness by becoming familiar with your spiritual home.

❖ Your spiritual home has deep roots that reach down into the soil of your family history.

❖ Don't work at being normal; just strive to be natural.

❖ To be natural is to trust and respect who you are, and to let that self flow.

❖ Success is not measured in money and stuff, or in prestige or popularity, but in having paid honor to the idea of becoming the person God created you to be.

Chapter 13

What Is the Point?

In This Chapter

❖ How the spiritual reality is that life offers no certainties, guarantees, or warranties

❖ Why at some point you will experience a spiritual bottom, a dark time of the soul

❖ How the spiritual journey must go down before it can come back up.

❖ What the point to all this is

"What is the point?" I love this question. I hate this question. I am sick to death of this question. I cannot have a healthy, happy life without this question. So it goes. All spiritual journeys go in circles.

At some point, you will feel very down. Spiritually, this is called despair. You feel down about yourself, sick of your family, tired of your friends, bored with school, frustrated by church or synagogue, overwhelmed by expectations and demands. Frightened of the future, negative, cynical, bitter, confused, irritable, exhausted, full of worry, and empty of hope.

At these times, the question "What is the point?" is bound to be on your lips. When you hit rock bottom, you will hear an eternal echo, an echo that goes back to the very beginning of the human race—"What is the point?" At rock bottom, you hit the spiritual reality that life does not offer anyone any certainties, guarantees, or warranties. You bounce off the hard truth that your life is finite and that the boundaries of the game of life have yet to be drawn.

The spiritual journey is always down before it is up. It is a downward ascent. You must go down into the depths of your soul. You must have the guts to dig down deep into your thoughts, feelings, and beliefs. You must feel the presence of the absence of a point. You must enter a dark cave of doubt. You must face the spiritual fact that you do not know. Then, and only then, can you rise up and live your answer.

The Point Is Life

Just before the birth of Jesus, the world was a mess—maybe no more a mess than usual, but definitely a big mess. Everywhere there were wars, and mainly over religion. There was widespread hunger and disease. The rich took care of the rich. The poor became poorer. The people who thought they had found God acted as though they had lost Him/Her. Mental illness was thought of as demon possession, as were a host of other diseases. Evil was rampant. Hope was on the wane. Add to the mix a few earthquakes, floods, and your garden-variety plague, and you have a world in despair.

Bill's Bible

"Enjoy the little things, for one day you may look back and realize they were the big things."

—Robert Brault

The Bible tells us that the answer God gives to this sorry state of affairs is a baby. A little infant is born in a barn to an unwed teenage mother and a very skeptical father. God's answer to the world's despair is simple. It is more life.

When you are forced to go down deep inside yourself and ask yourself "What is the point?" you, too, will recover the wisdom to know that life itself is the point. You will realize that there is no way to have life on your terms and that you must accept life on God's terms. Life may not be going your way, but it is going, unfolding the way it should. You have no other choice than to jump in.

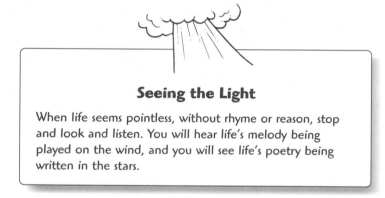

Seeing the Light

When life seems pointless, without rhyme or reason, stop and look and listen. You will hear life's melody being played on the wind, and you will see life's poetry being written in the stars.

When you hit bottom, for some reason you will be better able to see the big picture. Suddenly, the skies open and the sun begins to shine. You realize all the things about your life that you still enjoy, value, care about, and find precious. You realize that, in spite of all the crap it dishes out, life is still an amazing adventure, a wild ride, and a journey into joy.

When there seems to be no point to life, life points at life. Life asks you if you can see nothing beautiful in its face, nothing fine in its features, or nothing worthy of respect— even love. Life points at life and trusts that you will see there the answer that it can be and has always been.

In the Dark

When you feel that life has lost its point, it is really you that is lost. You have lost contact with your soul. You have closed your heart to love. You have closed your mind to the Word of God.

The Point Is Love

It saddens me when I hear my youth group talk about love. They speak of love with such blatant mistrust. They speak of it as if it is cotton candy you can't get off your hands—all sweet and gooey and pure sugar. They treat the subject with polite contempt, as if most of it is fake, forged, or counterfeit. Don't get me wrong—there is the occasional comment that expresses a genuine desire to be loved, or having found love, but a majority of the time, the topic of love arouses a most cynical attitude.

I'm not sure why that is, but I can make a few guesses:

1. Most adolescents know that the love they see on the movie and TV screens is either romantic fantasy or an all-out effort to destroy that fantasy.

2. Many of you have experienced the destruction of love firsthand, having learned well that vows are frequently made without serious consideration.

3. Your generation tends to expect people to be untrustworthy and disloyal. Although it is healthy that you have an appreciation for human flaws and failings, it is sad that this appreciation has become expectation.

4. No matter where you stand on the subject of premarital sex, I think you can agree that casual sex can create a climate of mistrust when it comes to love.

5. You live in a world of instant this and disposable that, so it is easy to think of love as something that you can have on demand or get rid of when you feel finished.

Bill's Bible

"In our life there is a single color, as on an artist's palette, which provides the meaning of life and art. It is the color of love."

—Marc Chagall

With all that said, love is still the answer to much of life's searching. Love can fill your soul. Love can inspire you to do important things and be a beautiful person. Love is best equipped to bring out the best in you. Love can melt a heart or remove its calluses. Love can change an attitude or transform a mood. Love can conquer despair or uproot evil. Love can make a miracle, create a vision, and give meaning to hope.

I have long believed that God is way too huge to fit inside one religion. I am quite content being Christian, but I remain interested and open to the wisdom of other religions. I am fascinated by how much the world's religions share in common. If there is one area upon which all religions seem to agree, it is that God wants us to love one another. The vital importance of love is at the core of every world religion. Although these religions may differ on how and where and why to express this love, they all fundamentally agree that without love, life would not be worth living.

Love is the point. It points to the most basic human drive and need. It points to an experience that enlarges our heart and deepens our soul. It points to the truth of our longing. It points to a genuine purpose. It points to a reason for being. It points to an enhanced living. It points to the poetry that can be written with our lives.

I think you know this point. I think that you have been stuck by the tip of this point. No matter how cynical or skeptical you may be, you still believe with your whole being that love can make the world go 'round and that you want to ride that carousel.

Ask yourself the following questions about the true status of your love life:

1. What do you love about your family? Dad? Mom? Brother? Sister?

2. Do you have a friend that you truly love? Why?

3. Do you have a friend that you find tough to love? Why?

4. Have you ever lost a significant love?

5. How did you handle that loss?

6. What do you love to do?

7. Are you presently in love? What is that like?

8. What do you love about your life?

9. What do you value most about a loving relationship?

10. What have you learned from love?

11. How would you define love?

12. Are you seen as a loving person?

13. How might you become a more loving individual?

14. Do you feel that you know the love of God? How?

15. What does it mean to you to love the world?

16. How do you need to be loved?

17. Have you ever been wrong about love?

18. Have you ever been wronged by love?

19. What can be wrong with love?

20. How can you get love right?

Bill's Bible

"Only love can be divided endlessly and still not diminish."

—Anne Morrow Lindbergh

God Is the Point

Although I have been a minister to youth for more than two decades, I still find the subject of faith and God to be awkward. The awkwardness, I contend, is the result of what you bring to the discussion. When it comes to talking about God, I experience most adolescents to have these traits:

✧ Afraid that they will be told what they must believe

✧ Suspicious of any conversation about God, and wary of being indoctrinated

✧ More aware of what they don't believe than in what they do believe

✧ Easily upset by any difference of opinion or belief

✧ Embarrassed by a lack of Biblical knowledge

✧ Uncomfortable claiming what they do believe, because they don't want to be thought of as fanatics

✧ Unsure of where to begin to look for faith

✧ Wrestling with a tragedy that has soured them on God

✧ Wrestling with all the evil in the world, which makes God seem irrelevant

✧ More comfortable with science and technology, where the answers seem certain and the results have immediate application

When you go down deep inside, face the certainty of life's uncertainty, and realize the limits of your own existence, I believe you have looked into the eyes of God. In those eyes you will see staring back at you an unconditional look of love, respect, and forgiveness. You will know in your heart that you are believed in. You will know in your soul that God has a plan for your life—and if not a plan, at the very least, a point!

I remember being on a flight home from London to Chicago, when we hit a terrible patch of turbulence. It was scary. I found myself praying to beat the band. I noticed the ashen faces of other passengers and was sure that they were praying as well. Now, I know that you might say this is just instinct, and in many respects you would be right. Danger and death confront us, and we start praying away. Still, I think that it speaks of something larger and is making a much bigger point. I think the point is that when there is nothing left to do but pray, we are declaring our hope that what is left is a God who cares about us.

I happen to believe that there is a God, and that my God cares infinitely for me, for others, and for the world as a whole. On almost a daily basis, I experience my life running to the edge of a cliff, only to be left with nothing else to do but take a leap of faith. Each and every day I am faced with the fact that I am not God, not in control, and not in charge; that there are no black-and-white answers; and that the only certainty is the illusion of certainty. That is why they call it faith. Faith is the ultimate trust.

A Leap of Faith

Kurt was a magnificent musician, poet, artist, and philosopher. Rarely had I seen such gifts in someone so young. For a long time, those gifts lay dormant. Kurt rarely played his music, painted, wrote poetry, or allowed anyone to experience his wisdom. He kept his parents off his back, his friends at bay, his teachers in the dark, and me at a significant distance. He was just Kurt, the nice guy who didn't do or say much.

Bill's Bible

"Some things have to be believed to be seen."

—Ralph Hodgson

In his junior year, Kurt fell in love with Kelly. Kelly was a spectacular young woman, a math whiz, and a potential concert pianist with a heart the size of Canada. Kelly did not just love Kurt—she believed in him. She embraced him with that belief—grace. She surrounded him with confidence. She affirmed him. She critiqued him. Her every word and action declared her belief.

Suddenly, Kurt was creating music. He wrote a magnificent collection of songs and joined a fairly well-known local band. His poetry was published in the school literary magazine and was entered in a couple contests. His artwork sold. He was exhibited in a fine local gallery. He gave a powerful address as valedictorian and gained entrance to Julliard.

It was Kelly's belief in Kurt that finally enabled Kurt to believe in himself, to take a leap of faith and begin to actualize his abilities. Without that belief, I am afraid that no one would have seen his gifts.

Belief can make the invisible visible. Belief can bring out the best. Belief inspires and motivates. Belief creates courage, confidence, and conviction. Belief shouts "Yes!" even when the world shouts "No!"

Pointers

There are no maps to the point. The point is not a buried treasure. The point is as obvious as life, love, and God. I cannot give you directions, but I can give you some pointers. Pointers will help you recover your own point. Pointers will enable you to discover the wisdom you carry within you.

These pointers need to be followed closely or not at all. You just can't dabble in the spiritual life; you have to become a serious student. These are some assignments that I believe every serious spiritual student might want to try:

- ✧ Keep a journal. A journal is not a diary. It does not record the facts of your day, but it records feelings, thoughts, beliefs, and experiences.

- ✧ Make prescription cards. If you had a great day, write down why. Call them prescription cards—whenever you get the blues, give yourself one of them.

- ✧ Keep a scrapbook of favorite memories—it is an attempt to remember what matters.

- ✧ Chase beauty around with a camera.

- ✧ Write poetry about life's toughest questions and subjects.

- ✧ Write yourself a letter. Ask a friend to mail it to you in six months.

- ✧ Write a creed, a concise statement of what you believe.

- ✧ Write your own personal 10 commandments, not about what not to do, but what to do and be.

- ✧ Write a sermon. Tell the world what you think it needs to hear.

- ✧ Keep a journal of prayers.

- ✧ Keep a journal of favorite quotes.

- ✧ Read a devotional book or a book of poetry.

- ✧ Read the writings of the mystics.

- ✧ Explore another religion. Develop an internal dialogue between that religion and your own.

- ✧ Interview as many people as you can on what they believe to be the point of life—their lives.

✧ Artistically try to create a symbolic portrayal of what you believe is the point of life.

✧ Attend a variety of worship experiences.

✧ Create a worship experience; invite your friends to participate.

✧ Create a worship experience with and for your family.

I believe that God believes in you. I believe that if you believed that, the world would see the goodness and beauty of who you are. Your gifts would be revealed. Your talents would be encouraged, developed, and devoured by a world waiting to receive them. Your life would become richer, fuller, and finer—as would your world.

One leap. One ounce of faith. One bit of trust. The flight begins, and oh how good it will feel to see you soar.

The Least You Need to Know

✧ When you hit rock bottom, you begin the ascent to the point.

✧ The only way back up is to get back into life.

✧ The only way to give life to life is to love.

✧ The only way to love life is to trust in the Creator.

✧ A leap of faith is a flight made on the wings of trust.

✧ To take a leap of faith, you must first spread your wings, and that means to respect and believe in yourself.

Chapter 14

How Can I Find Love?

In This Chapter

✧ Why the love of your family is the introductory course to the art of loving

✧ How friendship is the studio for working on the art of loving

✧ How intimacy is created out of time, trust, and truth, and is protected by a thick wall of forgiveness

✧ Why you aren't ready to fall in love until you are capable of intimacy

If spirituality is a journey, love is its destination. If spirituality is a subject, love is the course in which you must earn the degree. If spirituality is a way of life, then love marks the path. If spirituality is where you will find all of life's questions, love is where you will find life's answers.

Love is an art that requires discipline. It is an art that requires you to steadily develop your skill and own unique style. If you are serious about becoming a spiritual person, you will take the art of loving seriously. You will recognize that love represents your quizzes, tests, evaluations, and grades in the subject of spirituality. You will know in your heart whether you are passing. You will know in your soul whether you are failing. The spiritual goal is to graduate from The Art of Loving course with high honors.

Family: The Introductory Course

Your family teaches the introductory course on loving. Your parents are the primary teachers, but several classes will be taught by your grandparents, uncles and aunts, siblings and cousins, and even nieces, nephews, and in-laws. It is a course that lasts all of your childhood and through much of your adolescence. In some respects, it is a lifetime course. This is a course where you will receive no grades, but parents/family will be evaluated on a pass/fail basis. It should be what is called "an easy A" class.

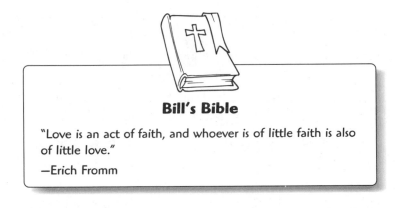

Bill's Bible

"Love is an act of faith, and whoever is of little faith is also of little love."

—Erich Fromm

If your parents are up to the task of teaching the art of loving course, they will give ample demonstrations on …

✧ The importance of good communication.

✧ The importance of affirmation and praise.

✧ The importance of respect and trust.

✧ The importance of forgiveness.

✧ The importance of having a sense of humor.

✧ The importance of speaking the words of love.

✧ The importance of doing the deeds of love.

✧ The importance of physically showing your love.

✧ The importance of honesty.

✧ The importance of boundaries and borders.

✧ The importance of responsibilities and consequences for failure to fulfill those responsibilities.

✧ The importance of unconditional loving.

If your parents are not competent to teach this course, it's probably because their parents failed the course or dropped out. However, almost all parents can at least do a good job on one or two of the lessons. If that is the case for you, take what you can learn, and get the other lessons from other families or friends or trusted adults. Although the art of loving should be a take-home course, if that can't happen, the course can be done by independent study. If your parents are trying to teach the course but lack the skill or expertise, again you must try to get the information elsewhere.

If you have had great teachers, count your blessings. If you have had lousy teachers, play it smart and find some good tutors. Do not give up on the course or on your own innate ability. No matter who taught the class, or how bad the teacher was, you are still capable of being an excellent artist.

In the Dark

A family and/or home that is filled with the secret of abuse, whether alcoholism or incest or physical violence, will not be able to hold classes on the art of loving. The course will be cancelled, and in its place, classes in survival will be held.

Friendship: The Studio Course

When you were a little kid, relationships were built almost exclusively from compatibility. You made friends with those kids with whom you shared interest or talent. Although you had to learn the art of sharing and playing nicely together, not much more could be taught. Compatibility was the glue that kept those relationships together; as interests changed, so did the relationships.

Friendship, on the other hand, is when you have moved on to the studio in order to work on the art of loving. Friendship is where you will learn how to do some serious art. Friendship is where you will develop your own style of loving. In this studio, you will let yourself play around with different styles. You might even copy a few. You will explore different techniques and see what works for you. You will explore many different media and find which ones feel most comfortable for you—and by which you can best express your individual art.

In the Dark

If all your friendships are still exclusively shaped by compatibility, you will know a lot of loneliness, no matter how many friends you have or how busy you are with them. That loneliness is a cue that you need to move to a deeper level of friendship.

The studio of friendship must be a place of genuine freedom. It needs to be a safe place, a sanctuary. It must be a place where much can be tried and mistakes can be made, a place for exploration and adventure, a place for acquiring discipline and skill, and a place of trust where you can cut loose and experiment.

Communication

Real friends communicate. They should communicate easily, often, and well. An obvious goal of friendship is to know and to be known. It may be scary to be known, but not nearly as scary as feeling unknown. The more you know and are known, the closer you feel. This closeness is the result of sharing the real you.

A good friendship is built upon mutual communication. A sharing that goes both ways. A good friendship should be comfortable sharing ...

- ✧ Wants and needs.
- ✧ Hurts and disappointments.
- ✧ Victories and defeats.
- ✧ Joy and sorrow.
- ✧ Other friendships.
- ✧ Time together and time apart.
- ✧ Different points of view.
- ✧ Ideas.
- ✧ Feelings.
- ✧ Some selected secrets.
- ✧ Dreams and goals; wishes and wants.
- ✧ Morals and values.

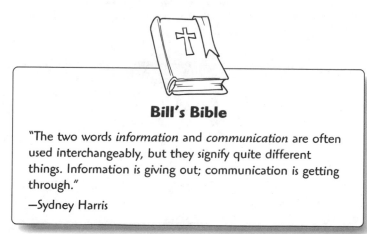

Bill's Bible

"The two words *information* and *communication* are often used interchangeably, but they signify quite different things. Information is giving out; communication is getting through."

—Sydney Harris

Spirituality is learning to communicate with your own soul. Spirituality is developing a friendship with your soul and your God. Spirituality is to resume contact and to keep close touch with your heart.

To have friends with whom you share your heart and soul can only enhance your spirituality. A good friendship is one in which you feel at ease sharing your inner world and feel safe releasing the messages of your heart. In a good friendship, two friends freely and frequently share with one another the journey of spirituality, the challenges of being real, the courage required to be fully human and fully alive, and their respective callings to live lives that inspire hope.

Compromise

When you were little, if a kid did not want to do what you wanted to do, you would often just leave. Sometimes your parents would make you stay and play, but truth be known, you were likely not to come back. If you didn't have anything in common, if you liked to play with and at different things, the relationship was pretty much kaput.

Maturation requires friendship. You cannot mature alone. Spirituality and maturation are often one and the same. Friends encourage maturation. Friends deepen your spiritual life. One sure sign of maturation is the ability and willingness to compromise. You are growing up as a person when you are willing to give in to some extent and to make a decision that is of benefit to two rather than one.

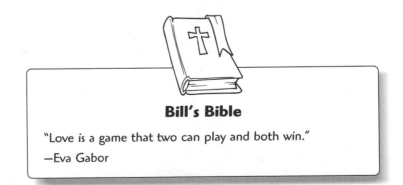

Bill's Bible

"Love is a game that two can play and both win."

—Eva Gabor

A compromise is a mutual decision, a mutual sacrifice, and a mutual bending of the individual will in favor of the friendship. It is giving a little to gain a lot. It is believing that whatever the loss to *my* way, is not nearly as important as the gain of *our* way.

What enables compromise to occur is the belief that the other person's way or idea is worthy of as much respect as your own. This belief is a declaration that you find the other person to be worthy of the same respect that you feel you deserve. This is an enormous spiritual step because the spiritual journey is one that will ultimately require frequent trips outside the self.

In the Dark

If you always have to have your own way, you will be going that way alone.

Confidence

The more time you spend in the studio, the greater confidence you will develop in your art. You will become sure of your ability to find a friend, make a friend, and be a friend. You will also grow more skilled in choosing friends. You will learn to choose friends with which communication is easy and relaxed, and with which going deep produces little anxiety. You will find compromise feeling less risky, with more to gain.

In a good friendship, you feel secure in sharing confidences. In other words, the confidence you feel in the friendship is justified by your ability to lay everything out on the table. A good friendship expects honesty. A good friendship enables revelation. You feel comfortable revealing your sadness, suffering, and secrets. You feel safe sharing that side of you that feels most fragile, The most easily hurt, and the most wounded.

As the confidence grows, so does the sharing and the caring. The confidence frees the love to flow. The love digs even deeper. The heart is opened. The soul is revealed. True intimacy begins.

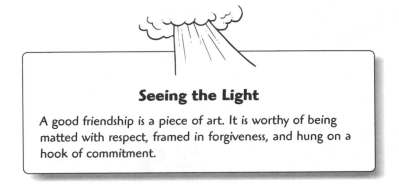

Seeing the Light

A good friendship is a piece of art. It is worthy of being matted with respect, framed in forgiveness, and hung on a hook of commitment.

Let me tell you a little about my best friend, Bob Shober. He has been my best friend for almost 30 years. We have not seen each other in four years, but he remains my best friend. That is the way with best friends—even at a distance, they continue to offer exactly what you need. Bob is my best friend because …

- ✧ He inspires me and gives me hope.
- ✧ He makes me laugh harder and longer than anyone.
- ✧ He cares about my history.
- ✧ He has shared much of my history.
- ✧ He listens to my stories and complaints over and over again.
- ✧ He forgives me when I neglect the friendship or act neglected.
- ✧ He gets me to play, to wonder, and to use my imagination.
- ✧ He asks me important questions.
- ✧ He never imposes his beliefs or values, but he does share them.

✧ He gives me gifts (not as great as the ones I give him, but he's still learning).

✧ He remembers me on important occasions.

✧ He goes with me through my losses and shares his own.

✧ He affirms me.

✧ He sings my praises to others.

✧ He is carefully critical.

✧ He makes me think and feel deeply.

✧ He makes the world a better place by being in it.

✧ He makes me proud to have him as a friend.

✧ When we won a play-writing contest and then he took and spent all the prize money without my knowing it, he let me forgive him. (Okay, I just don't want the guy to completely sound like a saint!)

Here is a rather brief questionnaire about your friendships. Hopefully it will help you clarify some of your attitudes regarding friendship, which friends are truly your best, and how you might be a better friend. Remember, a best friend is that someone who makes you feel relaxed, at ease, and free to be your real self.

Friendship Questionnaire

Complete the following sentences.

1. I think the most important quality in a good friend is ....

2. The friend who possesses this quality to the greatest degree is ... because ....

3. If I have a problem or am in crisis, I would probably go to ... because ....

4. I need a friend to be honest with me about ....

5. When I am really down, I need a friend to ....

6. I have betrayed a friend by ....

7. I have been betrayed by a friend when ....

8. I would be a much better friend if I would learn to be ....

9. I can always forgive a friend if ....

10. I think loyalty in a friendship is ....

11. As a friend, I am strongest at ....

12. I think friendship is built upon a foundation of ....

13. To be a good friend requires ....

14. There can be no friendship without ...

15. I regret losing my friendship with ... because ....

Intimacy: The Advanced Course

Intimacy is friendship thickly coated in love. Intimacy is a friendship in which both souls experience healing and hope as a direct result of the relationship. Intimacy is filled with insight and honesty—a mutual sharing of the real self. Intimacy is a friendship that has gone deep, penetrated to the spiritual core, and brought up many precious items to treasure.

Bill's Bible

"Intimacy means 'into me see'!"

—Bob Handel

Intimacy is an advanced course in the art of loving. Ample time must first be spent in mastering basic style and technique before you are ready for genuine intimacy. If you have worked long and hard on your art, it will someday reveal your soul. So it is with the art of loving. Intimacy occurs when you are ready to risk ...

- ✧ Letting yourself be fully known.
- ✧ Letting someone hold your fragileness in the palm of his or her hand.
- ✧ Letting yourself be seen emotionally and spiritually naked, and possibly physically.
- ✧ Letting someone inside, and letting yourself be deeply touched.
- ✧ Letting someone know you so well that you no longer feel any need to protect yourself or play games of any kind.
- ✧ Letting your soul speak.
- ✧ Being all of the above for someone.

To get to this point, you'll need the key ingredients: time, trust, truth, and forgiveness.

In the Dark

Beware of instant intimacy. Too close, too fast is always dangerous. Without the test of time, there can be no genuine trust—and without trust, the potential for disaster remains incredibly high.

Time

Intimacy is not easy. It does not happen overnight. It is never the result of a crush or an infatuation. Even love at first sight, which may occasionally occur, cannot claim it. Intimacy requires ample time. It is a long process of knowing. It is a lengthy effort at deepening. It requires commitment. It requires endurance. It is carved out of the stuff of life: ups and downs, successes and failures, times of sorrow and joy, closeness and distance, life and death, and even disappointments and betrayals. Intimacy must develop a tough hide, and that toughening can occur only over time.

There is no such thing as an instant artist. Nobody is talented enough to produce high-quality art with no real practice or time spent developing skill and style. Maybe someone might crank out one beautiful piece of work without much effort, but a sustained career demands long-term commitment and consistent effort. In the art of loving, where the art can never be just cranked out and a sustained career is always the expectation, even more time and effort will be required.

Trust

Trust is to intimacy and love what a brush is to a painting. Without trust, the knowing, the caring, and the sharing cannot be painted upon the canvas of the relationship. You may have everything else you need to create a beautiful piece of art, but without the brush, nothing can be applied.

Bill's Bible

"The best proof of love is trust."

—Joyce Brothers

You know the importance of trust: Your heart has taught you. It is devastating to have a friend break your trust. It is such a wonderful relief to know that you have someone in whom you can entrust anything. Trust enables intimacy to occur. It provides the sense of safety. It grants the atmosphere of security. It gives the gift of unconditional love without strings or expectations.

Truth

Intimacy has no time for being false or phony. It cannot stomach anything artificial. It has a taste for only the truth. You can't pretend to be an artist. A copy is not a work of art; it is a forgery. A piece of art that does not reveal the artist's soul is no better than some cheesy print you might buy at a garage sale.

In love, only truth can create a real work of art. Only honesty can feed the insatiable appetite of trust. Only honesty can fuel the creative juices. It is the truth, a rigorous honesty, that unleashes the power of intimacy to heal and transform, to make new, to shed light and wisdom, and to create faith, hope, and love.

Forgiveness

Even the best of friends can disappoint and fail you. We are all human. We are never perfect. A truly intimate friendship, one that has stood the test of time and in which the trust is strong and the foundation honest, is always capable of forgiveness. In an intimate friendship, the trust is so deep that it has several layers of forgiveness in reserve.

A friendship where you have swapped stories, lives, and souls is ready to forgive because the investment is so high and the dividends are so rewarding. A mistake by such a friend can be weathered because the friendship has known so many beautiful days. A bad storm is definitely seen as the exception to the rule. It would take a major catastrophic storm to destroy such a relationship.

Romance: The Exhibition

When you are capable of intimacy, you are ready to fall in love. Unfortunately, you may have fallen several times before you grew skilled in the art of loving. That isn't a bad thing—that is a sad thing. It just means that those romances were probably brief, and fairly unproductive. They may not have done much damage, but they probably didn't help much, either.

Although falling in love can be exhilarating, even addictive, it can become pretty dull having to pick yourself up again and again. Some folks think a long string of romances is a good thing. I disagree. I think it can kill your trust in love and ruin your capacity to do the work of intimacy. If the fall itself is the highlight of the relationship, it just isn't much of a relationship.

In the Dark

If a romance is always looking backward, trying to recapture the first feelings and experiences, it is already over.

I think of romance as an exhibition. This is where you get the chance to display your work in the art of loving. You are invited to show your skill and style in intimacy. You are being asked to reveal your heart. You are being given the sacred opportunity to make public the wisdom of your soul.

A romance is where you get to exhibit ...

✧ Your passion and compassion.

✧ Your tenderness and mercy.

✧ Your visions and dreams.

✧ Your deepest wants and needs.

✧ Your desire to be known and to know.

✧ Your need to heal and be healed

✧ Your drive to inspire and be inspired.

✧ Your personal statements of faith, hope, and love.

✧ Your personal style of living.

✧ Your collection of nudes—the naked you on every level.

Marriage: The Sale

I know it may sound crass, but I think of marriage as the sale. In the art of loving, though, what must be purchased is the entire exhibit. You can't just have the exciting nudes or the fascinating impressions. You have to buy the whole package: the early drawings, the preliminary sketches, the wild abstracts, and the sculptures and collages. This is an all-inclusive sale.

Marriage needs to be the pinnacle performance of your art. It is the museum where you hang only the best you have to offer: your insight and depth; your absolute honesty, trust, and respect; your willingness to forgive; your vows of commitment and loyalty; and your promise to keep creating. The friendship keeps deepening, the intimacy keeps expanding, and the romance keeps flourishing.

Making love is fun. It is play. It is also sacred communication. It can be divine. Within marriage, making love becomes all that it was intended. Marriage offers the confidence and security that enables love-making to express an intimacy that feels like heaven come to Earth. Marriage contains making love. The container is the promise of endless grace— unconditional love and forgiveness.

Marriage is the hardest work I have ever done. It is also the most rewarding and the most satisfying. I cannot imagine my life without my wife, and I love that feeling. Although it is a feeling filled with risk—the risk of someday losing it—it is a risk that gives life a good goosing. And that, my friends, was exactly what my life needed.

Bill's Bible

"Bitterness imprisons life; love releases it. Bitterness paralyzes life; love empowers it. Bitterness sours life; love sweetens it. Bitterness sickens life; love heals it. Bitterness blinds; love anoints the eyes."

—Harry Emerson Fosdick

"How can I find love?" I want you to live this question. If you fail to do so, your heart will turn bitter. Your soul and your life will be barren. This question will move you in all the right directions. The journey taken by this question promises to make stops to find good friends, to experience intimacy and romance, and to check the map for how to find a soul mate. It promises to be a real adventure—take it!

The Least You Need to Know

✧ Your family offers you your first course in the art of loving.

✧ If your family fails to offer the course or does a lousy job teaching it, take it by independent study.

✧ Friendship is the studio where you practice the craft of love.

✧ Intimacy is the choice to reveal the soul. This requires total trust and honesty, and a forgiveness guarantee. It takes real skill that can be acquired only over time.

✧ Romance should be an exhibition of all you have learned in the art of loving.

✧ Marriage is a choice of soul mates, a commitment to lifelong intimacy, and a vow to keep changing the exhibits to keep things fresh.

Part 5
Living Your Longings

Living your longings is a spiritual task. A spiritual life listens to the soul, especially when it shouts. The soul shouts, even screams when necessary, your longings. The soul is informing you of what matters most to you; what is the truest wish of your soul; what in your heart of hearts; what you most hope and dream.

To live a longing is to follow. It is to be obedient. It is to stay in line, as long as that line is being drawn by your longings. To follow your longings yields freedom. When you are obedient to your longings, you free your Self to be who you were created to be. You are choosing to become the person God wishes you to be.

The soul does not often shout. The soul is not a nag. You must learn to listen to your soul. You must learn the messages of your heart and the callings of your soul. You must pay your closest attention, however, to your longings. Your longings will grant you wisdom and lead you to happiness and joy. Longings. They alone can guide you down a path to peace—inner peace, outer peace, and peace of heart and mind.

Chapter 15

The Longing for Home

In This Chapter

✧ How homesickness can teach you about the spiritual power of the concept of home

✧ Why staying in balance is a vital step in finding the path home

✧ Why you need to do your homework to get back home

✧ How homing devices can help you find your way

✧ When and whom to ask for directions home

If Dorothy had never gotten to leave Oz and return to her home in Kansas, the story would have been a tragedy. If E.T. had never gotten to go home, Spielberg's masterpiece would have fallen flat on its cinematic face. If Lassie had never come sprinting back home each episode, the show would have bombed. Even as an audience, we identify with the longing to go home. We identify with it so much so that we are even willing to identify with a dog, an alien, and a little girl who plays with a lion, a tin man, and a scarecrow.

Your spiritual journey is destined to take you home. Home is where you can locate the real you. Home is where you will learn the art of loving and the skills of intimacy. Home has rooms available for your heart and mind. Home keeps the best room for your soul. Home is where God often dwells.

Home lies within you. The longing for home is built in, as natural as breathing in and out. If you refuse the journey, you will not be lost; you will simply be stuck on a dead-end road. You must travel to this home inside you. You must get familiar again with its many rooms. You will need to settle in and settle down. You will need to make it your own. To come home is to come home to your soul, to your true self, and to the God who created you.

In the Dark

Our whole world is battling homelessness. America not only has the physically homeless on its streets, but we also have the spiritually homeless hiding in their homes. Spiritual homelessness occurs when you have lost touch with your soul, your God, and you haven't a clue as to what matters, why to bother, where to head, or how to get there.

All longings are adventures. Following your longings is as risky as following a star. The longing for home is the greatest adventure of all because it is the one that promises to take you back where you belong.

Homeostasis

Homeostasis is a scientific term. I am lousy at science, so what I understand of homeostasis is limited. I know that it is the natural tendency of the body to find balance—like with your body temperature, for instance. If you have been exercising a great deal and are over-heated, you will sweat, right? Sweat cools the body. Sweat brings your temperature home to 98.6°F—balance achieved.

From a spiritual perspective, homeostasis is the soul's divine instinct to keep your whole being in balance. The soul is ceaselessly trying to inform you of when you are getting yourself out of balance. The role of the soul is to sound the alarm, to warn you when you are losing your God-given balance. If you lose your balance, you fall. So it is on an emotional and spiritual plane, only this kind of fall can do greater and more long-term damage.

Let's take a look at how you get out of balance physically, emotionally, and spiritually, and how the soul seeks to warn you.

You will get physically out of balance if you ...

- ✧ Get too much or too little sleep.
- ✧ Eat a diet that is not balanced (too many sweets, too much caffeine, no fresh vegetables, and so on).
- ✧ Exercise excessively or are a real couch potato.
- ✧ Binge-eat or drink alcohol.
- ✧ Experience excessive stress or anxiety.
- ✧ Try to do and be too much.
- ✧ Receive no physical affection.
- ✧ Be promiscuous.
- ✧ Feel uncomfortable with your sexuality.

You can get emotionally out of balance by ...

- ✧ Hiding from your fears or being a worry wart.
- ✧ Feeling consumed in guilt.
- ✧ Feeling overwhelmed by grief.
- ✧ Living in denial.

✧ Failing to forgive.

✧ Refusing to admit your need for love.

✧ Refusing to let yourself feel empathy or compassion.

✧ Obsessing about a relationship.

✧ Dwelling on a past mistake.

✧ Trying to control the future.

To be spiritually out of balance is to ...

✧ Lose your point.

✧ Wander away from your goals.

✧ Lose touch with your longings and callings.

✧ Lose touch with your heart and soul.

✧ Grow alienated from your true self.

✧ Grow alienated from the earth and life as a whole.

✧ Grow alienated from God.

✧ Become someone you are not—a phony.

✧ Become someone who only keeps others happy.

✧ Have no tolerance for being human.

✧ Have no tolerance for diversity.

The soul offers warnings. Just like a washing machine, the soul lets you know loud and clear when the load you are carrying has made you go out of balance. The soul will go to any length to get your attention, to let you know that you are not being yourself and that you've wandered away from home. You will not be able to function properly until you regain your physical, emotional, and spiritual balance. Here are some of the soul's warnings:

✧ You get headaches, neck aches, or stomach aches. Aches that have no other source than the soul are telling you that the load is too heavy.

✧ You become ill.

✧ You get cranky and irritable. Your temper flares. You have frequent outbursts.

✧ You get depressed. You feel frozen solid on the inside.

✧ You get mean and nasty. You take things out on somebody else. You find a scapegoat. You push someone else
down to try to get yourself back up.

✧ You become abusive of yourself, of others, or of sub-
stances.

✧ You get stuck in worry, in grief, or in guilt.

✧ You feel sick and tired all the time of everything.

✧ You feel empty, alone, and isolated.

✧ You feel dead inside.

These soul warnings might sound harsh. They are, and they
are meant to be. This is the soul fighting for its life and your
life. At times, the only way for the soul to restore your balance is to first knock you flat on your physical, emotional,
and spiritual butt. When you hit bottom, then things can
start looking up: You will start looking up your soul and your
God again, getting back in touch.

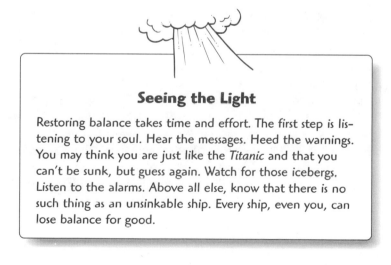

Seeing the Light

Restoring balance takes time and effort. The first step is listening to your soul. Hear the messages. Heed the warnings.
You may think you are just like the *Titanic* and that you
can't be sunk, but guess again. Watch for those icebergs.
Listen to the alarms. Above all else, know that there is no
such thing as an unsinkable ship. Every ship, even you, can
lose balance for good.

Homework

When you lose your balance, God will add insult to injury by giving you some homework. This homework is aimed at helping you learn how to restore your own balance.

Homework is indeed work. It's not easy, but it is meant to make you stronger. This homework is God's lesson on how to come home to your real self, how to restore your balance, how to get back on track, and how to feel calm again and at home in your own skin. When you lose your balance, you feel queasy, anxious, and out of sorts, but this homework promises to settle your spiritual stomach.

Daily Devotions

Some people think of daily devotions as a time of prayer and Scripture reading. That is a good definition. If you did just that every day, you would have satisfactorily completed your homework. However, daily devotions can mean many different things. This can mean devoting time and energy to cultivating a talent or gift, performing a service for others, learning something new, experiencing something fully, or doing some form of self-improvement.

There are two words here. Each one carries a key message: First is *daily*. This means that you need to make a consistent effort every day. You need to accept your homework as a ritual. Second is *devotions*. The message in this word is that you must offer a heart, mind, and spirit that are focused. You can have no distractions and nothing else demanding or draining your energy. *Daily devotions* is to choose to do what you feel matters. It is to do that which you believe enables you to be your best. It is to spend time and energy in such a way that the investment will pay God a handsome dividend.

Here are some wonderful suggestions for daily devotions:

✧ Keep a journal.

✧ Write a poem or a thank-you card.

✧ Choose a good devotional book, and read.

✧ Meditate

✧ Do yoga.

✧ Take a walk—have a chat with your soul.

✧ Experience nature—have a chat with Creation.

✧ Give order to a mess.

✧ Do a favor.

✧ Visit a person you know needs a visit.

✧ Paint, sculpt, dance, draw, or create your art.

✧ Choose a movie that will make you think and feel.

✧ Reminisce. Recount your favorite things.

✧ Plant something, and care for it.

✧ Recycle.

✧ Go for a bike ride.

✧ Find a quote that holds meaning for you.

✧ Take a photo of the most beautiful thing you see.

✧ Make a genuine sacrifice.

✧ Attend worship.

✧ Pray with someone.

✧ Make a meal. Serve a meal. Clean up after a meal.

✧ Just listen.

Bill's Bible

"Discipline is remembering what you want."
—David Campbell

Loosen Up

Your homework will also include emotional calisthenics. You
need to free up what you feel. You need to jar loose those
feelings that are either buried or stuck. If you are to be able
to spiritually come home, you will have to have a flexible
heart. A flexible heart is unafraid to claim what it feels and to
learn from those feelings. Emotional calisthenics will get the
heart warmed up and ready to run the spiritual race. When
the heart is loosened up, it is ready to receive the many messages that God and life have to offer. Emotional calisthenics
are nothing more than the following:

✧ Claiming feelings

✧ Naming feelings

✧ Feeling feelings

✧ Listening to feelings

✧ Learning from feelings

Lighten Up

Another key assignment in your homework will be to do
some spiritual jogging. By exercising the soul, you will enable
yourself to shed more light on the subject. Spiritual jogging is
the discipline of awareness, of noticing, and of paying attention. As the soul expands consciousness, you will move out
of the shadows and into a more enlightened state. Spiritual
jogging is letting the soul run free, which is to become more
aware. Spiritual jogging is the exercising of the soul, so that
the soul will ...

✧ Take notice of the gifts of the day.

✧ Take note of the messages of the body.

✧ Pay attention to Creation.

✧ Pay attention to others.

✧ Become more aware of the world around you.

✧ Become more aware of the world within you.

✧ Expand your consciousness.

✧ Live in the light rather than in the dark.

Homing Devices

Pigeons have an internal homing device that calls them back home. Well, in this case, you are the pigeon and the homing device is of a spiritual nature. A spiritual homing device is something that you can use to bring you back home to your self. A homing device can get you back in touch with your center, your callings, and your longings. A homing device is a simple "trick" that wise folks use to get their acts back together. If you are falling apart, these devices can restore the whole you. If you are losing balance, feeling awkward and ill at ease, these devices can help you regain your composure and sense of calm. If you have fallen, these homing devices can help pick you back up.

Lasers

Home is not just a place. It is an experience. It is a mood and atmosphere, a perspective and attitude, a way of being. When it is functioning as it should, home is where you feel this:

- ✧ You truly belong.
- ✧ Your life has meaning and purpose.
- ✧ You are safe and secure.
- ✧ You can relax and be yourself.
- ✧ You can be ugly—homely, physically, and emotionally.
- ✧ You know your place and know rules, roles, and rituals.
- ✧ You don't have to prove anything.
- ✧ You have unconditional acceptance.
- ✧ You can really laugh and cry.
- ✧ You feel loved, wanted, and needed.
- ✧ You have a group of defenders.
- ✧ Your soul can be found and feels safe.
- ✧ You feel most in touch with God.

Beauty Is a Homing Device

There is a reason why so many folks stop to notice a sunset: It is just so beautiful. That beauty calms you. It restores balance. It makes you feel at home in the universe. I think that for many of you, it restores your faith in a Creator, or at least that Creation is indeed a miracle to behold. No matter how many times you see a sunset, it is just as beautiful. Each one is unique. Each one is awe-inspiring. Awe is guaranteed to bring you home and reunite you with your soul. It will get you back in touch with God. Stay open to awe!

Intimacy Is a Homing Device

You have just had a deep, honest conversation with a good friend. You have gotten a lot off your chest. You have vented some pain. You have shared a secret. You have swapped a few dreams. You feel so much better. You feel so relaxed. You feel at home in your own heart, mind, and body. You feel like you are back to being your real self. You are home! The act of sharing your self with someone who is close to you is always an excellent way to bring you back to *you*.

Silence Is a Homing Device

Peace and quiet. The absence of noise. Silence is beautiful, like the kind you find sitting on a comfy stump in the middle of the woods, or on a blanket at the beach under the stars. The silence speaks. The silence is never really silent. The silence tells the tale of truth and weaves the story of your soul. Just as is the case with all good yarns, it brings you back where you belong to the best that life has to offer and the best that you can be. Good stories always inspire. The soul is inspired by being back home.

Prayer Is a Homing Device

Prayer is an attempt by the soul to focus: to focus on the needs of others and the world, to confess one's own needs and flaws, to give thanks, to ask for assistance, and to request that a burden be removed. Prayer is a focused effort to establish contact between the human spirit and the Holy Spirit (the Higher Power). Prayer is conscious contact with God. The act of choosing to pray brings you home. The act of prayer is a choice to go home. Prayer is a return to your center, to come back to the genuine core. Even if you feel that God did not answer your prayer, or even if the answer to your prayer was no, what truly matters is your choosing to open your soul to God's presence. Prayer extends an open invitation to God: "Please visit. Please come home."

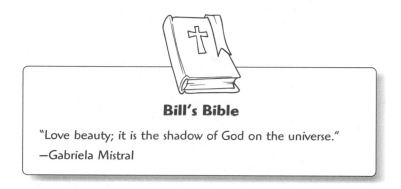

Bill's Bible

"Love beauty; it is the shadow of God on the universe."
—Gabriela Mistral

Service Is a Homing Device

Service is doing. Service is doing for others. Service is doing for others without expectation of gain. Service is doing for others because it is simply the right thing to do. Service is being humble enough to know that you are not above serving anyone.

Service brings you home to these truths:

- ✧ You are no more special than anyone else.
- ✧ When you choose to serve, you ultimately help yourself.
- ✧ Acts of service are reminders that you are a child of God and that you are a member of the human family.
- ✧ Acts of service defy our culture's wish that we do nothing without getting something in return.
- ✧ Doing something for nothing can give you everything.
- ✧ The service entrance always leads back home to the soul.

Worship Is a Homing Device

Worship is an experience. It has many parts, but each part seeks to bring you home to your self and to God. Worship involves the singing of praises, the confessing of sins, the hearing of Scripture, the listening to a sermon or meditation, the prayers of comfort and hope and thanksgiving, the giving of offerings, the receiving of blessings, the joining with a community of faith. All parts head home. There is no other goal or destination in the worship experience. All worship is homeward bound.

Doing Nothing Is a Homing Device

I believe strongly in the need to take a few free days each month. By a free day, I mean a day that has no duties. This is a day free of tasks, chores, or responsibilities. It's a day to play, a day of grace, and a day without any expectation other than to experience it. Just do it. Just live it. Just enjoy it. Taking a free day is what our culture calls doing nothing.

Doing nothing is probably the best homing device you have at your disposal. What makes doing nothing such an excellent homing device is ...

- ✧ It underscores the fact that you are not in charge or in control.

- ✧ It makes you humble, and humility restores the soul.

- ✧ Play helps you to rebuild your spiritual home.

- ✧ Doing nothing is living life to the fullest—only this time, it is full of doing and being what you love.

- ✧ Doing nothing brings you home to the truth that you are entitled to receive God's grace.

- ✧ Doing nothing frees you to be true to your self and to be true to the will of God for humans to be human.

- ✧ Doing nothing is to become God's playmate for a day.

- ✧ Doing nothing means trusting God to fill the day with whatever you need—to fill your spiritual home with love.

Mentors Are Good Homing Devices

At times, you just get so lost that you cannot even find your way back home. When this happens on a spiritual basis, you may need to pay a visit to a spiritual mentor. Good spiritual mentors will give you the directions or a map, or take you home themselves. A good spiritual mentor is someone you trust with your heart, someone who inspires your soul, and someone you will allow inside your spiritual home.

If you remain lost for a significant period of time, and if your traditional mentors are just not doing the trick, you may need to seek out a professional spiritual mentor. Get recommendations from people you trust. Try to find someone you believe is competent and compassionate, and cares about getting you home.

The Least You Need to Know

✧ Homesickness can leave you paralyzed because the longing for home is so powerful.

✧ You need to feel physically at home in your own skin, emotionally at home in your heart, and spiritually at home in your soul.

✧ Your whole being—heart, mind, body, and soul—is striving daily to maintain your balance. All your parts offer you clues, cues, warnings, and signals.

✧ When you are knocked off balance, God will give you the homework needed to teach you how to regain your balance.

✧ Homing devices help you regain balance.

✧ Beauty, intimacy, silence, prayer, service, and worship, coupled with doing nothing and seeking mentors, can all help bring you back home.

Chapter 16

The Longing for a Calling

In This Chapter

✧ Where your calling comes from

✧ Why you need to pay attention to the gathering of voices affirming your innate abilities.

✧ How to follow your calling

✧ How your calling helps you live a truly spiritual life

I was leading an adult retreat at a camp on a lake in Vermont. It was near the end of a long day, and I needed a retreat from the retreat. I went out to the end of the floating pier and promptly fell sound asleep. When I finally awoke, it was pitch black. A wind had arisen and was rocking the pier, and when I turned around, I realized that I could not even make out the shore.

I am a lousy swimmer. I do not like deep water. I did not know how deep the water was at the end of this pier. When I stood up, the pier was rocking so badly that I sat right back down. I froze in fear. I didn't want to yell for help. That, I felt, would not be manly and would only call attention to my stupidity and fear—an unbeatable combination.

I suddenly heard a voice. It was my good friend, Judy. She yelled "Grimbol, is that your big butt out there?" I told her it was. I didn't give it to her for the not-so kind reference to my pudgy anatomy—I was too overjoyed from hearing her voice. She told me to come in. I told her of my anxiety. She laughed but then told me to kneel and crawl to shore, and she would lead me with her voice. That is what I did. It was humiliating, but it got me to shore. It got me exactly where I passionately wanted and needed to go. Once on shore, we laughed and hugged. I had to admit, it was pretty funny.

I think that a calling is just like that. You wander off. You fall asleep. You wake up in the dark. You are anxious and afraid. You don't know how to get back to the point of your life. You feel stranded on a floating pier—out on a limb. The lake has been made choppy by the winds of fashion and popularity. You don't know how to return to the soul's shore. You long for that shore. You yearn to be back where you belong and where your feet feel steady. You are dying to get back on track.

Suddenly, you hear a voice. It is a foreign voice. It is a familiar voice. It is a voice that speaks out of the silence. It is a voice that becomes a map, guiding you back home. It is a voice that calls you back to your purpose, meaning, and destiny. It is a voice that enables you to envision life on shore.

That voice is your calling. That calling is your direction. That calling will free you to flow. That calling will enable you to make your mark. More importantly, it will entrust you with the responsibility of putting God's signature upon the skin of your own existence.

The Inner Voice

If I am working with children six and under, and I ask them what they think they are good at or what they like about themselves, the answers come like an avalanche. I am a good artist. I can ride a pony. I do ballet. I'm smart at math. I'm a good tumbler. I won a spelling contest. I can jump really high. I have 46 dead bugs in a box under my bed. They go merrily on and on. You have to stop them, or they would just keep going and going, like that battery bunny in the TV ad.

If I ask the same kids the same question, only a few years later, the answers come in drips. Most of the kids bow their heads. They don't make eye contact. They fidget in their seats. Maybe one or two kids will say something, but even they do so in a whisper.

What happened? It is the inner voice. Somehow, the inner voice that was once bloated with pride and a sense of talent and giftedness is now muted in shame. The inner voice has been drowned out by other voices that say:

✧ Don't be a bragger.

✧ You aren't all that talented.

✧ You are not that special.

✧ You need to improve.

✧ You need to work harder.

✧ You just aren't good enough.

✧ Let me show you where you are wrong.

✧ Let me show you your mistakes.

✧ Maybe you *are* the mistake.

At a very young age, the inner voice is muted by a din of negativity and criticism. Kids are made all too aware of what they lack and how they've failed. Even if their grades are excellent, they still have heard so much about what is wrong with them and have witnessed how humiliating it is to be wrong in our culture that they soon learn to stay quiet. They don't take any chances. They play it safe. They keep others happy. Thus, the inner voice grows hoarse and can barely be heard.

The inner voice is the soul speaking. The soul gives gracious messages. The tone of the voice is gentle. The sound is inspirational. The soul, the inner voice, is always speaking to you of your calling. The soul is asking you to take note of these things:

✧ Your natural talents

✧ Your God-given gifts

✧ Those things you do that give you the greatest pleasure

✧ Those things you do that give you a deep sense of satisfaction

✧ Those things you do that enable you to lose track of time

✧ Those things you do that help make you a better person

✧ Those things you do that make the world a better place

✧ Those things you do that bring out the best in others

✧ Those things you do that give you hope

✧ Those things you do that make you jump for joy

✧ Those things you do that bring joy to God

Seeing the Light

The inner voice offers you positive messages filled with faith, hope, and love. Even those messages that are critical are spoken in a kind and gentle manner. The goal of the inner voice is never to frighten by excessive volume or to shame by excessive force.

The inner voice speaks incessantly about those things. The inner voice tells you what truly matters. The inner voice reminds you of what gives a sense of worth and value. The inner voice encourages you to do those things because those things all belong to God. Those things come together as your calling. They are your call to make a difference and a mark, to leave a legacy. They form a blessed opportunity to write your name across life's heart.

The inner voice gives only messages of good news. Ironically, it is the good news that you have trouble hearing. It is the announcement that you are good and beautiful and worthy of respect. It is the request to take seriously your own creative powers. It is the acknowledgement that you are filled with light, and that the darkness is no more than your shadow. It is the good news that makes you feel awkward and anxious. But it is the good news that you most need to hear. The inner voice speaks this good news, like a pulse or a metronome.

You are God's partner, friend, and co-creator. God is calling upon you to know this and to live this truth. God is asking you to fulfill your calling, to add light to the world and to be a seed of hope. God is telling you on a daily basis that you not only matter, but that you matter to God. God loves you. How simple. How elegant. How true. It is this love that gives shape and form to your calling. It is this love that gives vision to a calling first uttered by your inner voice.

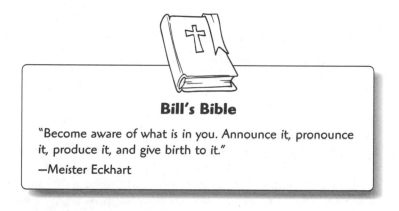

Bill's Bible

"Become aware of what is in you. Announce it, pronounce it, produce it, and give birth to it."

—Meister Eckhart

A Gathering of Voices

Do you pay attention to compliments? Do you take note of praise? Do you let yourself receive positive affirmation?

Over the years, you will begin to hear a gathering of voices.

These voices form a verbal bouquet of affirmation. These voices will inform you of your talents, or in what you are considered to be naturally gifted. If you are listening and absorbing the message, you will begin to hear an echo. Over and over again, you will be hearing the same thing. You are repeatedly hearing positive acknowledgements of particular skills and abilities that you possess. It is these particular aptitudes that folks continuously highlight.

Over the years, you will begin to hear a consistent message that calls your spiritual attention to ...

- ✦ How you shine.
- ✦ How you inspire others.
- ✦ How you amaze.
- ✦ How you make an impact.
- ✦ How you are uniquely gifted.
- ✦ How you have a natural talent.
- ✦ How you were born with certain aptitudes.
- ✦ How you are a genius.
- ✦ How you create memories.
- ✦ How you create something eternal.
- ✦ How God appears to be working in you.

These are the markings of your calling. This is the aura that surrounds the choice to follow a calling.

Now, why wouldn't you hear this gathering of voices? Well, in truth, many of you choose not to hear them. You do so because you may consider the oft-mentioned ability not to be worthy of praise. You may feel your talent is insignificant, or its field unimportant. Some of you disown a talent because you have been told there is no money in it or that you will not be able to make a living at it. Trust me, you will all make a living. By the world's standards, you will make a very good living. The real issue is whether you will *enjoy* a living. That is dependent on being true to these talents and gifts—your calling.

Many of you are quite dismissive of your natural gifts. You are told that you are a real "people person," sensitive, insightful, kind, and yet you don't really believe that this matters. It does. It is tragic not to take seriously your gifts and talents, even when seemingly abstract. You may not get a grade or a paycheck for being a "people person," being good with children, having a green thumb, or having good common sense, but you will get to have an enjoyable life.

The Voice of God

God's voice is not huge. It is not a thunderclap. Still, it is a distinct voice. It is an unmistakable voice. It is a calm voice in the midst of a storm. It is a quiet voice that can be heard only by those wise enough to listen to the wind. God's voice is always telling you some important things:

- ✧ That you are fine and in good hands
- ✧ That life is unfolding as it should
- ✧ That life is well worth living
- ✧ That the best way to live is by loving
- ✧ That you must live in such a way that your love is maximized
- ✧ That you must love both what you do and who you are
- ✧ That a loving life is a full life
- ✧ How to do acts of love
- ✧ How to be love itself
- ✧ How to be true to your self
- ✧ How to be true to your calling
- ✧ That you are called to be human
- ✧ That you are called to love
- ✧ That you are called to share your own special gifts and talents
- ✧ That you are called to live as an artist and to create your particular art with devotion, discipline, and drive
- ✧ That your art is your calling and your bit of genius

I am a minister. I am called to ministry. So are you. You are called to minister to others, to the Earth, to the world, and to and for God. Your ministry, like mine, is how you choose to make the world a better place. Your ministry is how you demonstrate your love. Your ministry is how you help and heal the earth and its inhabitants. Your ministry is the message you live and the legacy you leave. Your ministry is how you bind broken hearts, make peace, breed respect, and sow the seeds of mercy and justice. You are a minister. You are ordained by God to give your best to this world.

In the Dark

Ministry is a helping profession. It involves helping yourself and others to be human and to celebrate that humanness. You most likely think of yourself as someone who needs no help. If you think that you need nobody's help, you may need more help than you know.

I am an ordained Presbyterian minister. I never saw a burning bush or had some mystical encounter with Jesus. I never heard God speak to me from a mountaintop. However, I am vividly aware of God's presence. I can feel it in my bones. I can hear it in my head. I can sense it in my soul. My heart quivers when God is near.

God's presence speaks to me. I can feel God's presence calling me to be honest, fair, just, tender, merciful, passionate, and courageous. I know when God is near. My whole being tells me. I just have to listen to my life. My life is telling me where God wishes me to go. God's presence arrives whenever I am to note a situation that speaks of something that truly matters. God shows up when I am wrestling with what to do or how to be. God is there when it counts, when it is something of lasting value.

I have also heard God's absence. I know when I have chosen to disobey God's will. I feel lost, empty, lonely, and ashamed. I am incapable of joy. I am not at peace. I feel wired and whirling. I feel out of balance. I feel alienated. I am spiritually homeless. God's absence also speaks loudly and clearly.

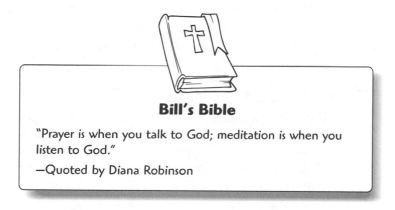

Bill's Bible

"Prayer is when you talk to God; meditation is when you listen to God."

—Quoted by Diana Robinson

Some folks call this your conscience. Some call it your morality or ethics. Some even call it the human condition. I'm not uncomfortable with any of those definitions of the voice of God. All I know is that God speaks. The voice rings true and reverberates off your heart, mind, and soul. Some truths you just cannot deny. Even when you try, your tears, that lump in your throat, or those goose bumps will prove to you once again that you have heard from God.

Think of your future in terms of ministry, and complete the following questions and sentences. Your answers will help illuminate your spiritual calling.

My Ministry

1. What does it mean to you to be a minister?
2. What are the skills required of a competent minister?

3. What are the personal attributes of a good minister?

4. How will you try to minister to others?

5. How will you try to minister to the earth?

6. How will you serve as a minister in the world?

7. I would describe my own personal ministry as ....

8. In terms of ministry, I am lacking in ....

9. If I am to be the kind of minister of which I am capable, I will need to work hard at ....

10. I think God wants me to minister through my ....

Giving Voice to a Vision

The longing for a calling is the longing to have a purpose. It is the deep desire to feel that life not only has a point, but that the mark you will make will be eternal. To know one's calling is to feel in touch with what you believe God has set for you to do and to be.

The spiritual life offers only one doctoral degree, and that is in the field of calling. Calling is vital to the spiritual life. If you fail to follow your calling, you will have failed to be the person God created you to be. You will not be fully real. You will not be fully alive. You will not be hopeful. You will be travelling a well-worn path that goes nowhere.

A calling comes from God and is heard within. It is a voice that gives vision. Now you can see life's rhyme and reason. You can see where you are headed and why. You can see the meaning in your existence and claim your own worth. You can see the future and approach it with confidence and creativity. A calling enables you to be aware of what ultimately concerns you and to live a life that will voice those concerns.

You are called. You are called to be a special presence and to do special things. You are meant to have a life that has meaning. You are meant to be true to your God-given purpose. You are meant to enjoy life and to create some joy. You are meant to make your mark, to make a difference, and to be an original. You are meant to know that you are uniquely loved and believed in. And you are meant to know that you are called to a spiritual life, a life that celebrates the myriad gifts of being a human being.

Lasers

✦ Your calling is your ministry.

✦ Your ministry is your purpose.

✦ Your purpose is to love.

✦ Love is the point.

✦ The point is to love and live to the fullest.

✦ You are full of God-given talent and ability.

✦ You are meant to use your gifts.

✦ Your gifts offer your life meaning and give glory to God.

✦ God keeps on calling—hoping you will hear and pick up. God always dials direct.

The Least You Need to Know

✧ Your inner voice deep within your soul is informing you of your calling.

✧ The message of your inner voice is echoed by a gathering of voices, all of whom acknowledge and affirm your talents and gifts.

✧ A calling comes from God and asks only that you give back to the world those gifts that you have graciously been given.

✧ A calling gives voice to a vision of your future and tells how you might minister in your own particular way.

✧ The longing for a calling is a burning desire to believe that your life has a point and a purpose.

✧ The longing for a calling is the means by which God writes His/Her signature upon your soul.

✧ The longing for a calling is how God in turn grants you the sacred responsibility of writing your signature upon God's own heart—life.

The Longing to Live Life to the Fullest

In This Chapter

✧ Why settling down does not mean you have to settle for less than your dreams or to cease dreaming

✧ How to live life to the fullest by bursting at the seams—bursting with pride, bursting with ideas, and bursting with love

✧ Why risk is essential to living a full life

✧ How change is the author of most maturation and spirituality, and thus, the creator of a full life

✧ The ways in which celebrating gives life a dimension of fullness

The following story is a composite of what actually occurred in the lives of three different young men. The thrust of the story is the same in all three lives, but the composite characterization enables me to maintain confidentiality.

Edgar was a great kid. He was in my first youth group. He looked like a Norman Rockwell painting—red hair, freckles,

Chiclets for teeth, and a scarecrow body. He loved to laugh, and he spoke with a booming voice. He was always in motion.

As a sophomore, Edgar was a decent student with a well-known passion for theatre and for travel. He played the leads in *Our Town, The Music Man,* and *The Diary of Anne Frank.* He was mesmerizing on stage. He was such a presence of raw energy. He inhabited a character. When he talked about travelling, his whole face would light up. Although the farthest he had ever gone was Toronto, he spoke constantly of his dreams to visit India, Japan, and China.

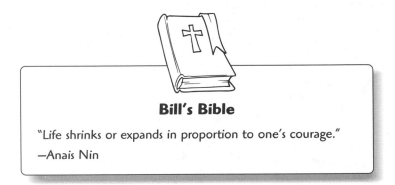

Bill's Bible

"Life shrinks or expands in proportion to one's courage."

—Anais Nin

Edgar also had a huge heart. He was the kid who always made sure our youth group visited the sick and shut-in, as well as the nursing homes. He got us involved in picking up and delivering used clothing to a Lutheran Resale Shop in downtown Milwaukee. One of his goals was to serve in the Peace Corps, and he frequently mentioned that he would love to make that his whole career—just moving from country to country to serve others. Obviously, for a youth minister, this kid was a dream come true.

During Edgar's junior year, his father ran off with a neighbor, who was also married and the mother of four. The scandal was huge. The impact on Edgar's family was devastating, especially financially. Edgar was forced to move with his mother and sister to a small town in northern Wisconsin, to live with his grandparents. The school Edgar attended his senior year had no theatre department, and he claimed in his letters that most of the kids there did not know China existed. At the end of Edgar's senior year, his grandfather died of a massive stroke, and Edgar was installed as the head of the family.

That was more than 20 years ago. Last year I received a phone call. The voice on the other end was soft and halting. I had no idea who it was, and embarrassingly I had to ask for a name. It was Edgar. He was still living in the same town. He was married, had a child, and continued to care for his mom and grandmother. When I asked him if he was doing any theatre, there was absolute silence on the line. I asked if he had gotten to do any of the travelling he had hoped. Again silence. My heart sank when I realized that Edgar was crying.

I affirmed him for all his efforts to pull his family together, and I praised him for his many sacrifices. He thanked me but said that the reason he had called me was to see if I might ignite some old sparks. Now I was silent. I told him that a good place to begin would be for him to come east for a visit. I said I would treat to half the plane ticket. He needed to talk it over with his wife and family, but he thought it sounded fine.

Edgar got off the plane at La Guardia. He looked exactly the same. His spirit, however, was dying a slow death. He was hesitant, almost shy. He was difficult to talk to and added little to the conversation. It was like being with a carcass, a shell of a man that had once housed a most magical boy.

He loved being in Times Square. He laughed like I remembered when he saw the size of his Stage Deli sandwich. He was ecstatic after seeing a matinee performance of *Rent*. That night as we drove back to my home in Sag Harbor, we talked at length about the loss of his dreams. It was painful. It was clearly a relief for Edgar to talk about it, but he said repeatedly that he had to accept his fate—settle in and settle down.

I was careful. I did not want to inspire any dreams in him that would also meet a swift demise. I told him that there was nothing wrong with settling down, but that he had settled down so low that I would have to pipe light to him. He laughed. I told him that he must hang on to at least some of his dreams, or he would wind up living a life that always felt somehow empty.

This story does have a happy ending. Edgar started a small local theatre company and serves as its director. It isn't Broadway, but it is theater, and even he admits that he is a great teacher. He also is saving for a trip to India with his wife and child. They have set up a savings account, and his mother surprised and pleased him by making a major contribution to it this past Christmas. The last time I spoke with Edgar, he sounded happy and alive. His life may not be as full as he had hoped, but it is full enough.

One thing is for sure: Had Edgar given up on his passions, and had he removed them completely from his life, he would have been dead before he was dead. His spirit would have shrunk and shriveled to the status of waste. Having a full life does not mean having or getting everything you want, or fulfilling all your hopes and dreams. It does mean having a life that fulfills enough of your promise, ambitions, and dreams that you can feel satisfied.

Settling

You, too, will have to settle. You will have to accept your boundaries and borders. That is called maturity. The issue is when, where, and how you settle, and for how much. You must decide whether you are settling for less than you deserve, or dream, or hope to accomplish. You must choose the timing of settling. You must face the challenges forced by refusing to settle.

I have never liked the notion of settling down. That implies that getting married, having a family, going to work, and being a friend and neighbor is somehow a downward motion. I think not. I believe that my best experiences in life have been the result of ordinary, day-to-day family living and being a plain old ordinary minister. Settling down for me has been a most uplifting and expanding experience.

Bill's Bible

"It's only when we truly know and understand that we have a limited time on earth—and that we have no way of knowing when our time is up—that we will begin to live each day to the fullest as if it was the only one we had."
—Elizabeth Kubler-Ross

To me, the real issue is settling for less—less than you had hoped, less than what you are capable of, and less than God expects. Edgar's life was not bad; it was just empty. He had settled for the elimination of his passions. That was way too much. Yes, there are times you will have to settle for less, but that must not become a way of life, a perspective, and an attitude. A good settlement should be a win/win situation.

You will know that you are settling for less than you deserve and must expect, if these are true:

✧ You are living out someone else's dreams.

✧ You keep everyone happy but you.

✧ You have given up on that which gives you satisfaction.

✧ Your life has no joy in it.

✧ Your life always feels somehow empty, like there's a missing piece.

✧ You are bored to death.

✧ The rut you are in is at grave depth.

✧ You wake up feeling sad.

✧ You go to bed feeling sad.

✧ You have stopped setting goals.

✧ You have ceased dreaming.

✧ You never include yourself in your prayers.

✧ You doubt that your life is pleasing to God.

You are responsible for keeping your dreams alive. You must make sure that you never let the flames of your passion go out. You must find the sparks that ignite your longings. Nobody can give you a full life. Nobody can fill you up, not even the great love of your life. Nobody but you can see to it that your life is being lived with enthusiasm and energy.

A full life is the direct result of a full effort.

Life has limits. You must settle, and even settle down. You must face the reality and unpredictability of death. The choice is whether you run and hide, or run and live. You can either shrink from the challenge or fill yourself up with courage and sign up for the race that God has set before you. To be spiritual is to run that race. To be spiritual is to be unwilling to hide. To be spiritual is to refuse to shirk your responsibility to give life all you've got—the fullness of who you are.

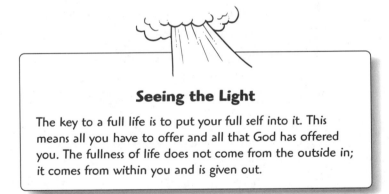

Seeing the Light

The key to a full life is to put your full self into it. This means all you have to offer and all that God has offered you. The fullness of life does not come from the outside in; it comes from within you and is given out.

Bursting

Sadly, many of you think of bursting as a bad thing. You think of destructive explosions. When you are bursting at the seams, you feel anxious and worried about the outcome. You may hate movies that leave your head bursting with thought or your heart bursting with emotion. You may live in dread of bursting into tears. You don't want to be seen as all that vulnerable and all that human. Let me burst your bubble—you are!

Bursting is a good thing—anxiety, even worry, included. Those are just signs of life, of a fast flowing-pulse, and of a surging life force. These are the wings of a wish fluttering in your heart, and a dream taking shape in your soul. Bursting is to be on fire. Bursting is to be aroused by life. It means that you are full of the energy of God.

You know you are bursting when …

- ✧ You just can't wait.
- ✧ You can feel your heart pounding.
- ✧ You get excited just thinking about it.
- ✧ You can barely breathe.
- ✧ You feel like you could run a mile in a minute.
- ✧ Your brain feels on fast-forward.
- ✧ You greet the day with a leap out of bed.
- ✧ You collapse in bed at night, exhausted and spent.
- ✧ You feel on fire.
- ✧ You are one with God.

Bursting is to live with enthusiasm. It is to be possessed of an enthusiastic spirit. It is a feeling that there is not enough time in each day to savor all the beauty and goodness. It is the feeling that at the banquet of life, you are on your third helping.

Cynicism is to live without any enthusiasm. It is to be possessed of a negative and deadening spirit. It is to act as if each day is a drag, an endless battle to just stay awake. It is to refuse to come to the banquet of life because you believe that it is nothing but reheated leftovers.

Bursting or cynical? The choice is yours. It is a choice between a fruitful life or one that is rotten at the core.

Risking

Risk is essential to having a full life. You cannot get into the swim of things if you have to keep one foot permanently on shore. As an old fisherman on Shelter Island told me "A ship is safe in the harbor, Pastor Bill, but that isn't the reason why we build ships."

Bill's Bible

"If you risk nothing, then you risk everything."

—Geena Davis

Now, when I speak of risk, I don't mean taking dumb chances; I am not referring to driving a car too fast, downing flaming shots of booze, or running with the bulls. That isn't risk. That is stupidity masquerading as courage. I am talking about the need to take chances that can expand your life in positive and healthy ways, make you more alive, give you a better chance to demonstrate your gifts, and give you that fresh start you need. I am talking about ways to keep God happy.

A healthy risk is one that has these characteristics:

✧ Enables you to learn and grow

✧ Strengthens your sense of self-esteem

✧ Expands your talent

✧ Frees you to be more authentic

✧ Frees you to display your gifts

✧ Gives you the grace of a fresh start

✧ Allows you to discover new things about your self, your life, Creation, and God

✧ Grants the experience of adventure

✧ Tests your abilities and your courage

✧ Deepens you emotionally

✧ Forces you to mature spiritually

✧ Releases your compassion

✧ Releases your passion

✧ Releases your love

✧ Brings out the best in others

✧ Serves God

✧ Helps to build the Kingdom of God on this Earth

The primary reason that you fail to take risks is that you fear failure and/or embarrassment. For some of you, this is the fear of success: To be successful would place upon you the expectation of more success, and you may be trying to avoid that. If you do not overcome these fears and take the risk, the leap of faith, you will never know. Your life will be framed in a giant "What if ...?"

Life is full of risks. To get in touch with the risks, fill out the following questionnaire by completing these sentences:

Risky Business

1. I never risk doing anything that might ....

2. I took a foolish risk when I ...

3. At home I need to risk showing ....

4. At school I need to risk showing ....

5. At church/synagogue I need to risk showing ....

6. I would love to risk learning about ....

7. I would love to risk getting to know ....

8. I would love to risk letting people see ....

9. In friendship I need to take the risk of ....

10. In love, I need to take the risk of ....

11. In my life I hope that I will risk doing ....

12. In my life I hope that I will risk being ....

13. In my faith I need to risk ....

14. I consider it to be a foolish risk to ....

15. The person I have experienced as most courageous is ... because he/she ....

Seeing the Light

A risk is a chance. A chance is an opportunity. An opportunity is a gift. A gift comes from God. To receive that gift is a leap of faith. That leap is a real risk. A real risk is worth taking.

Changing

Picture this. I am in the midst of a marriage counseling appointment. This is what I hear:

"She has just changed so much. She is not the woman I married."

"I am, too."

"No, you are not. Your whole attitude is different."

"You mean, I don't agree with everything you say."

"You don't agree with *anything* I say."

"You're right. I have changed. I don't worship and adore you anymore, but I do still love you."

"It sure doesn't feel like it."

"That is your problem, not mine."

First, I always find it amazing when people are shocked by change. Of course his wife has changed. Did he want her to stay fixed at one point in time? Well, in this case, yes. He wanted his wife to stay the young woman who was madly in love with him, the woman who never questioned him or doubted him, and who certainly did not challenge him. Still, why would you want a spouse who stops growing? That is certain death for a marriage.

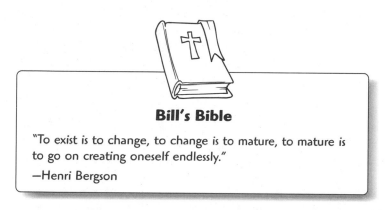

Bill's Bible

"To exist is to change, to change is to mature, to mature is to go on creating oneself endlessly."

—Henri Bergson

Second, change is often vital in keeping things fresh. In the case of this marriage, the husband would go on to learn that although he no longer had a wife who worshipped him, he did have a wife who was his friend, his partner, and a source of inspiration. Change is the fuel of so much maturation and spiritual growth. Admittedly, this couple went through some really tough times. Change can be brutal—but the result was a deepening and a strengthening of an already good relationship.

Change keeps life fresh. It expands our selves, our world, and our horizons. Change is the foundation upon which life is built. At first that might frighten you or make you feel that you are on shaky ground. Not at all. Every day you walk firmly upon a spinning planet, so it is with life. Change is like a spiritual conveyor belt—it is there only to make the walk a little easier and to take a load off your feet.

Life without change cannot be full. It will be forced to shrink.

In the Dark

Initially, change creates conflict. Some of you have severe conflict-avoidance. You will do almost anything to avoid the pain and anxiety of conflict. Conflict, however, is the mother of creativity, and the labor pains of that conflict will give birth to genuine spiritual growth.

Celebrating

Life is tough. It does take a lot of work. It is often filled with conflict and pain. It requires ample courage. Life can leave you drained, defeated, and spiritually deflated. Life can make you want to run and hide. Life can be a real bummer.

But life also is beautiful. You can become an artist in loving. It is full of rewarding events and experiences. It can make you so full of happiness, joy, love, and compassion that you feel ready to burst at the seams. Life can make you open to more and more. Life can be wonderful.

You will look at life from both sides. Some days you will want to close the door on life and lock it out. Other days you will swing the door wide open and invite life in. You will want to have more days like the latter than the former. You want a life full of days that make you glad to be alive. Now the question is, how do you choose to have those kinds of days?

I think that a full life is a choice. It is a choice not to settle for too little. It is a choice to take vital life-giving risks. It is a choice to change, to keep things fresh, and to move on under the power of forgiveness. Most importantly, it is also a choice to celebrate. A full life means to celebrate these:

✧ Who you are

✧ Where you have been and what you have learned

✧ The love you have shared and hope to share

✧ The blessings you have received

✧ The mistakes that have forced you to become more humble

✧ The losses that have tenderized your heart

✧ The defeats that have deepened your soul

✧ The moments of joy

✧ The ordinary miracles

✧ The treasure of friendship

✧ The gifts of love and sexuality

✧ The challenges of faith

✧ The acts of kindness, generosity, and service

✧ The tragedies shared in family and community

✧ The victories shared in family and community

A celebration is simple. First, it means setting time aside. Make the time feel and be special. Create a time and space in which to give thanks. Create an atmosphere conducive to rejoicing. Enjoy the chance to give yourself and those you love some credit. Give a big thank-you or gift. (I prefer gifts.) Mark the time with signs of specialness: special decorations, a special place, special people, and a special acknowledgement.

In family, friendship, and marriage, these mini-celebrations can give your life a real boost. They can lift the spirits and restore the soul. They can bring back your energy and enthusiasm. They can rebuild your hope. Such a celebration may be no more than five minutes, but that five minutes can fill up the next several weeks with love, joy, and a renewed passion—the full life.

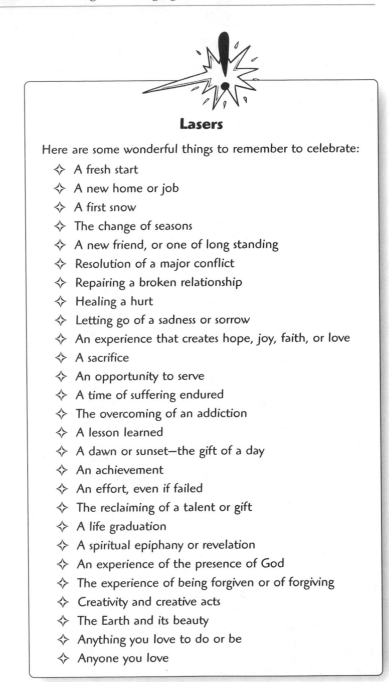

Lasers

Here are some wonderful things to remember to celebrate:

- ✧ A fresh start
- ✧ A new home or job
- ✧ A first snow
- ✧ The change of seasons
- ✧ A new friend, or one of long standing
- ✧ Resolution of a major conflict
- ✧ Repairing a broken relationship
- ✧ Healing a hurt
- ✧ Letting go of a sadness or sorrow
- ✧ An experience that creates hope, joy, faith, or love
- ✧ A sacrifice
- ✧ An opportunity to serve
- ✧ A time of suffering endured
- ✧ The overcoming of an addiction
- ✧ A lesson learned
- ✧ A dawn or sunset—the gift of a day
- ✧ An achievement
- ✧ An effort, even if failed
- ✧ The reclaiming of a talent or gift
- ✧ A life graduation
- ✧ A spiritual epiphany or revelation
- ✧ An experience of the presence of God
- ✧ The experience of being forgiven or of forgiving
- ✧ Creativity and creative acts
- ✧ The Earth and its beauty
- ✧ Anything you love to do or be
- ✧ Anyone you love

The Least You Need to Know

✧ It is fine to settle, but not if it means disowning your dreams, passions, or longings.

✧ Bursting at the seams is a spiritual experience. It means that you are ready to grow, learn, change, and become.

✧ A full life is full of change and requires some risk-taking.

✧ A full life is one that celebrates the little victories.

✧ If you are committed to a spiritual life, you will fill your life with those experiences that bring out your best, enable you to mature, force you to learn and grow, and challenge you to change.

Chapter 18

The Longing to Be Forgiven

In This Chapter

✧ Why forgiveness is the fuel of faith and the essence of a spiritual life

✧ Why you will need to be able to forgive yourself

✧ Why you will need to learn how to forgive others

✧ Why you will need to be willing to forgive God

✧ The ways in which forgiveness is hard work—but it is also a grace

My wife, Christine, was excited about her new job. She was beginning a chaplaincy program at a large metropolitan hospital. Her assignment was the emergency room. She told me that she was nervous, but confident. She was enthusiastic when she left home.

Late that night she returned. She looked pale and distraught. She explained that her first case had been a tragic teen suicide. She told me the following sad, sad story.

Jeremy was 14. He had a large nose. A group of four boys in his class had teased him unmercifully about his nose. They called him "hose nose" and "elephant nostrils." Over the summer, Jeremy begged his parents to let him have a nose job. His parents were a working-class couple, and a nose job was expensive. However, sensing their son's anguish, they saved the money and let him have the cosmetic surgery.

The first day of school, Jeremy was feeling quite proud. He went to school feeling happy. It had been a long time since he had felt that way about going to school. At school the same four boys were waiting for him. They began to chant "nose job, nose job." Jeremy burst into tears and sprinted home. He called his father at work and told him that if he didn't come home now, he was going to kill himself. Jeremy's father raced home, only to hear the gun go off as he pulled in the driveway.

Chris met several times with Jeremy's family. Jeremy's folks needed to forgive themselves for failing to pay attention to Jeremy's angst and not getting the surgery done at a much earlier age. Jeremy's older brother needed to forgive himself for not intervening with those four boys. The whole family needed to forgive themselves for failing to take Jeremy's pain seriously—sooner.

Chris was also asked to meet with the four boys. Although at first they tried to act macho and claimed that they could not understand Jeremy's overreaction, they soon were able to admit their deep guilt in knowing what their teasing had caused. After one such meeting with these four, Chris came home and said "You know, life is just one big, long adventure in forgiveness." Initially, I believed Chris' comment to be the result of dealing with an extreme situation, but after two decades of ministry, I have come to agree fully with her assessment. Life is indeed an adventure in forgiveness.

Forgiving Your Self

Here's the bad news: You make mistakes—big ones. You fail. You flop. You say some wicked stuff. You try to get even. You try to hurt someone's feelings. You act phony. You pretend to love. You pretend to be a friend. You have secrets. You have sexual secrets. You break vows. You betray a friend. You can disappoint your parents and those who love you most. You go against your own morals and values. You tease. You ignore the needs and pains of others. You can be totally self-absorbed. You can be arrogant. You lie.

Bill's Bible

"The day the child realizes that all adults are imperfect he becomes an adolescent; the day he forgives them, he becomes an adult; the day he forgives himself, he becomes wise."

—Alden Nowlan

Now here's the good news: You are human. We all do all of the above. You can change. You can improve. You also do all kinds of good stuff. You are remarkably kind and loving, generous and compassionate, courageous and full of conviction. You can be mature way beyond your years. You can rally in a crisis and be stronger and more loving than you ever thought possible. You can serve and suffer and sacrifice. You can be humble and tolerant. You can be forgiving. You can be honest to a fault.

Here's the sad news: You tend to focus on your flaws and failings. You are your own worst critic. You judge yourself harshly. You treat yourself poorly. You beat yourself up emotionally. You think of your sin as your soul. You feel like you are never enough. You feel that you are destined to become either someone you are not or someone that you don't want to be. You carry around all kinds of guilt garbage, which stinks up your whole life. You refuse to let go of your sins, and you cling to them. You think of yourself as a fake, and you can't believe that nobody has figured that out yet.

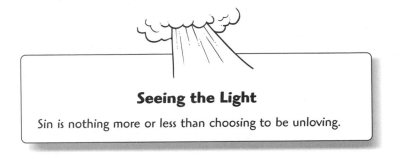

Seeing the Light

Sin is nothing more or less than choosing to be unloving.

Here's the glad news: You can learn how to treat yourself more graciously. You can befriend yourself. You can become a spiritual individual, committed to taking good care of your health and hope. You can become less critical of yourself. You can stop the relentless attacks on your self-esteem. You can choose not to listen to those who only put you down and never build you up. You can accept that God not only loves you, but has good reason for loving you. You are worth loving. You are also very much worth forgiving.

Forgiveness is a conscious choice and action. You must choose to forgive yourself, and that means you must claim that you are forgivable. Let me state my faith in this regard. There is nothing—*nothing*—you have done that falls outside the realm of God's grace. You can be forgiven. The issue is whether you will go though the long and often painful process of asking and receiving forgiveness.

Forgiveness is not just words. Forgiveness does not happen in the head. Forgiveness is a change of heart. If you are to be able to forgive yourself, you will first need to love yourself. If you believe that you are a bad person, then you will accept and expect yourself to be and do bad things. If you believe that you are a good person, you will strive to correct your mistakes and become the person you know you can be. Forgiving yourself is predicated upon the belief that you do love yourself.

Lasers

The steps of forgiveness, as I understand them, are ...

✧ **Step 1: Naming.** You are able to admit the offense.

✧ **Step 2: Claiming.** You are ready to take full responsibility for the offense.

✧ **Step 3: Confessing.** You admit your offense and your desire to be forgiven, to your self and to God.

✧ **Step 4: Remorse.** You are ready to address your desire for forgiveness to the person you have offended.

✧ **Step 5: Repenting.** You are ready to do the work of forgiveness.

✧ **Step 6: Changing.** You work at changing the offensive behavior.

✧ **Step 7: Transforming.** You work at changing the attitude that contributed to the offensive behavior.

✧ **Step 8: Receiving.** You open your heart to being forgiven.

✧ **Step 9: Surrendering.** You give the offense over to God. You let it go. It is gone.

✧ **Step 10: Forgetting.** Your soul functions free of that guilt.

These steps are rarely followed in order. They do, however, suggest the flow of forgiveness.

Forgive yourself. I mean that—do it. Take the time to address the sin, offense, mistake, or failing. Name it and claim it. Bring it into the light of day. Be aware of it. Make God aware

of it. Ask to be forgiven. Ask yourself for forgiveness. Ask
your God for forgiveness. Ask the person you have wounded
for forgiveness. Then do the work of being forgiven. Change
your behavior. Transform your attitude. Release the love in
you. Surrender the guilt. Move on. Forget about it. Remember
the power of being forgiven.

Forgiving Others

As a minister, I can honestly say that I am appalled at how seldom we who claim a faith in a forgiving God choose to forgive
or be forgiven. These words, *forgiving* and *forgiven,* are one and
the same. Yet most of us turn our back on both. Why?

✧ Because we cannot claim our humanness or their humanness

✧ Because we cling to guilt and secretly believe that the
   guilt is never enough

✧ Because we do not know how sorry is sorry enough

✧ Because we don't trust repentance to be genuine

✧ Because we still want to get even

✧ Because we want to see the other person suffer the way
   we have suffered

✧ Because we still believe in an eye for an eye

✧ Because we still want to be in control and resist turning
   anything over to God

✧ Because we resent God's graciousness

✧ Because we resent God's ultimate celebration of spiritual
   equality—especially God's refusal to rank sin and sinners

✧ Because it is easier to punish and get even

✧ Because dwelling in and on the guilt feels strangely
   good, like a tongue returning again and again to touch
   a chipped tooth

I cannot tell you how many marriages I have watched dis-
solve, simply because the couple was unwilling to do the
work of forgiveness. I can't believe how many families I
have seen destroyed by the refusal to forgive. I find it tragic

to witness friendship after friendship go down the tubes, simply because two people cannot forgive each other. It is amazing that most of us know and claim the centrality of forgiveness to faith and a spiritual life, yet are unwilling to meet its demands for discipline. We just don't do it! We talk the talk, but we do not walk the walk.

Bill's Bible

"Then Peter went up to him and said, 'Lord, how often must I forgive my brother if he wrongs me? As often as seven times?' Jesus answered, 'Not seven, I tell you, but seventy-seven times.'"

—Matthew 18:21–22

How about you? How many friendships have you ruined because you would not forgive or be forgiven? What grudges are you still carrying? How are you still trying to get even? How are you punishing someone for a sin committed long ago? What excuse do you give yourself for not forgiving others? What reasons do you give yourself for being in the right and for pointing out how badly you were wronged? Do you dwell on the wrongs committed against you? Do you find yourself hating the person who did you wrong? Do you think of your sins and mistakes as less than that person's? Do you think of yourself as a morally superior person to him or her?

If you find it tough to forgive others, ask yourself the following questions:

1. What are you getting out of clinging to your anger?

2. Ultimately, what do you hope your efforts to get even will produce?

3. If you chose to forgive, how would you change?

4. If you chose to forgive, how would God respond?

5. What price are you paying for carrying this grudge?

6. What repair work would have to be done in order for this relationship to heal? Are you willing and open to do that work?

7. If your trust has been broken, how does this person build back that trust? What are your terms? Have you spelled them out?

8. Are you open to negotiations or interested only in revenge?

9. How would you like to see this conflict resolved?

10. How do you determine whether someone deserves to be forgiven? Could you meet those same standards?

Forgiveness is a spiritual basic. You need to get back to the basics—we all do. You need to know that you have been forgiven again and again, many times without you knowing and many times without you deserving it. God asks the same of you—nothing more, nothing less. You are no better than anyone else. You are not above having to forgive or be forgiven. God's playing field is the same for all. Play ball! Forgive!

Bill's Bible

"If you judge people, you have no time to love them."
—Mother Teresa

Forgiving God

It may be odd for you to think of forgiving God, but there are times where I believe that is vital to your spiritual growth. I also happen to believe that God understands such need, and is "big" enough to handle it.

I have always marveled at the intimacy of the Old Testament writers with their God. They experienced such closeness that they had no trouble expressing their frustrations, doubts, and even rage at Him/Her. They truly thought of God as family, and therefore felt free to express everything, even those feelings that you might think God would find offensive.

Bill's Bible

"O Lord, how long will you forget me? Forever?
How long will you look the other way?
How long must I struggle with anguish in my soul,
with anguish in my heart every day?
How long will my enemies have the upper hand?"
—Psalm 13:1–2

I think many of you find it hard to forgive God for these things:

✧ The givens of a planet populated by free human beings: the evil that takes place in this world; the rapes, murders, and wars; the starvation; the homelessness; the torture and physical and sexual abuse; the ethnic cleansings past and present; the ongoing insanity of religious wars.

✧ The givens of nature: the reality of earthquakes, floods, tornadoes, hurricanes, volcanic eruptions, and avalanches of snow, mud, or water.

✧ The givens of your own body: too tall or short; too skinny or fat; short legs or a thick neck; big ears, nose, or feet; not pretty or handsome—enough; homeliness; physical disabilities; illnesses or disease; inherited disorders.

✧ The givens of your own being: not talented enough, or not gifted in anything you think is important; not all that smart; learning disabilities; inability to carry a tune or draw a stick figure.

✧ The givens of your family: too poor, or too rich; alcoholism or mental illness; divorce; sexual infidelity; emotional or spiritual abuses; pattern of worry or fear, or abundant shame.

✧ The givens of life: You will get sick; you will suffer; you will get your heart broken; you will know stress; you will go through some horrible losses; there will be accidents; there will be tragedies; you will die.

✧ The givens of God: unanswered prayers, or prayers that were answered with a "No"; His/Her absence or seeming indifference.

Forgiving God means coming to terms with these givens. It is to agree to accept God's terms. It is to know that you are not in charge or control, that life will not go exactly as you think it should. Forgiving God is ultimately surrendering to the truth that much of God's will and ways will remain a mystery.

Forgiving God is accepting your givens, or at least those you cannot alter, like height, or I.Q., or perfect pitch. It is a willingness to work within the perimeters of those givens and to do what you can with what you've got. It is also striving to change that which can be changed. If you are a terrible

￵speller, you can work hard at learning how to spell. If you have a black thumb, you can learn how to turn it green.

Forgiving God is the acceptance of going with the flow—God is that flow. It is renewing your trust that God does know where God is going. It is not just agreeing to go along for the ride, but choosing to enjoy the journey.

The Serenity Prayer, which is often used at Alcoholics Anonymous meetings, effectively states God's terms for life:

> "God grant me the serenity to accept
> the things I cannot change,
> the courage to change
> the things I can,
> and the wisdom
> to know the difference."

The grand irony here, is that when you forgive God, it is ultimately God who is doing the forgiving for you. God is forgiving God. I'm not sure I can make sense out of that. I think it is something you can accept only if you believe it to be true. It is a leap of faith.

Forgiveness Is a Work

The longing for forgiveness comes naturally. The actual forgiveness is a long and arduous task. The difficulty in forgiving and in being forgiven is that they both require entering a conflict, an open wound, and a painful experience. You cannot give or receive forgiveness without first laying claim to the conflict.

As I have said earlier, conflict does yield pain and suffering. Conflict does create worry, anxiety, and fear. Conflict rocks the boat. Conflict does not play it safe. Conflict creates temporary insecurity.

Bill's Bible

"Stop judging others, and you will not be judged. Stop criticizing others, or it will all come back on you. If you forgive others, you will be forgiven. If you give, you will receive. Your gift will return to you in full measure. ... Whatever measure you use in giving—large or small—it will be used to measure what is given back to you."

—Luke 6:37–38

Conflict, however, also creates maturity. It is responsible for most learning and growth. It is essential to all loving relationships. It is the acid test of integrity. It is the degree offered by dignity. Life without conflict is spiritless, a void that is stagnant, shallow, and deadening to the soul.

The work of forgiveness requires that you enter and resolve the following conflicts:

✧ The desire to get even, or to accept that God has left the score eternally tied

✧ The desire to see the other person suffer, or to be glad to see an end to the suffering

✧ The desire to punish, or the need for a fresh start

✧ The desire to make sure that person feels appropriately guilty, or the need to lift the shroud of guilt

✧ The desire to have someone rebuild your trust, or for you to share in the building

✧ The desire to cling to a wrong, or the wish to make things right

✧ The desire to hang on to a hurt, or to let it go to God

- ✧ The desire to keep a wound open and well-salted, or to spiritually strive to stitch it together

- ✧ The desire to show off your scar, or to have it removed by faith—it will hardly even show

- ✧ The desire to see the other person learn and grow from a mistake, or the wisdom that it is forgiveness that always has the most to teach

Forgiveness Is a Grace

Forgiveness is such hard work that you often cannot do it alone. I firmly believe that God must do it with or for you. Sometimes you must see another person through God's gracious eyes. You are just too full of hurt and anger to be able to forgive. You simply cannot muster the courage or conviction necessary to start the process.

What do I mean by letting God do the work for you? Again, I am not all that sure I can explain this, but I will do my best.

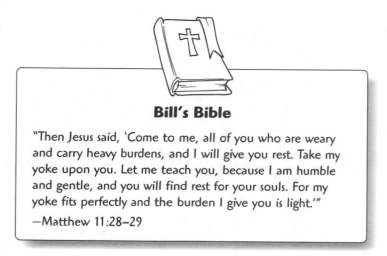

Bill's Bible

"Then Jesus said, 'Come to me, all of you who are weary and carry heavy burdens, and I will give you rest. Take my yoke upon you. Let me teach you, because I am humble and gentle, and you will find rest for your souls. For my yoke fits perfectly and the burden I give you is light.'"
—Matthew 11:28–29

When you are bloated with a need to get even, or when the wound remains wide and painful, you are not ready to forgive. At those times, you must bring the grudge to God, as you understand God. You need to pray about the matter. Ask for God's will and wisdom. Try to put God on like a cloak. You will find that God responds something like this:

- ✧ Reminds you of how often you, too, have failed or made a mistake
- ✧ Asks you to remember how frequently you have been forgiven
- ✧ Informs your heart of the futility of rage or the desire for revenge
- ✧ Informs your soul of the freedom to be found in forgiveness
- ✧ Informs your faith that you are being asked to forgive in His/Her name
- ✧ Informs your whole being that grace is contagious and can heal the world

Don't get me wrong. Your resistance to turning this process over to God will be mighty strong. You will find numerous ways to stall and avoid the issue. However, the fact remains that if you are serious about being a spiritual individual, then your new forgiving nature must be exercised on a regular basis.

All forgiveness comes from God. It works in you, through you, and in spite of you. All you need do is open your heart and mind to its presence. Let it in. Receive it. Let it out. The yoke that God asks you to wear is forgiveness. You wear it because you are human. You wear it because it is a gift from God. The burden God asks you to carry is to forgive others. But this is a light burden: It is far heavier to carry around anger and hurt than it is to embrace your spiritual responsibility to forgive.

Seeing the Light

Forgiveness is a grace. Think of a first snow: wet, white, and wonderful. A bleak and barren earth is now coated in magic. It can take your breath away. Where once the earth stood drab and dreary, it now shimmers with beauty and elegance. The grace that is forgiveness is like that snow. It coats us. It removes the old and worn out, the ugliness. It lifts up the goodness of life. It reminds you of the gentleness and kindness of the God who loves you with His/Her whole heart.

The Least You Need to Know

✧ You cannot be alive without needing to forgive and be forgiven.

✧ The job of forgiveness is yours, and there are no days off.

✧ The wage you receive for performing this job is the freedom to enjoy your life.

✧ If you cannot forgive yourself, you will certainly be unable to forgive others. This completes the spiritual circle. You give back what you first received.

✧ You will need to accept God's terms for living, and that will require you to forgive everyone—even God.

✧ The discipline of forgiveness requires that you first receive grace.

✧ Forgiveness is the grace of God. It is given freely and unconditionally. It is the yoke that you must wear to spiritually survive. It is a perfect fit.

✧ The only real burden you carry in life is that you are mandated to be forgiving. That is a light burden.

Index

M

N–O

P

T